HOME CANNING THE LAST WORD

NEWER AND BETTER METHODS FOR TOP QUALITY

By Louise W. Hamilton, R.D.
Gerald D. Kuhn, Ph.D.
Karen A. Rugh
with the Food Editors of FARM JOURNAL

D1468603

COUNTRYSIDE PRESS
a division of Farm Journal, Inc.
Philadelphia, Pennsylvania

Distributed to the trade by Dolphin Books
Doubleday & Company, Inc. Garden City, New York

Book Design: Maureen Sweeney
Cover Design: Alfred Casciato
Cover Photo: William Hazzard
Drawings: Suzanne Eagles

ISBN: 0-385-12454-6
Library of Congress Catalog Card Number 76-14041

Contents

Introduction

Every authority on home canning predicts a big season this year: more home gardens, more people canning for the first time and (our prediction) more questions than ever before about home canning!

Our work with county Extension home economists in Pennsylvania, and with homemakers, seeded the idea for this book. We are convinced that home canners—beginners as well as the more experienced—not only need information about basic canning procedures, but also a clear explanation of the *whys* behind canning successes and failures. And, of course, our aim is to provide the very latest research results available to insure home canned food that is safe to eat and of top quality.

This book includes instructions for canning common fruits, vegetables and meats, along with information on how and why to use certain equipment. And it explains fully why it is necessary to follow specific rules on super-cleanliness and heat sterilization methods and times.

Without exception, the experienced canners who have read the manuscript for this book say they've "learned a few things": for example, why foods darken or change color and what one should and should not do about it; how detergent residue in otherwise clean jars affects food color; how longer sterilization times for tomatoes insures their safety; how tight to tighten jar lids; why hot packed foods result in higher quality than raw packed foods; when you must use a pressure canner and how to use it properly.

And so here it is . . . the last word on home canning . . . with the most up-to-date information on such canning headliners as low-acid tomatoes and new jar lids . . . a careful and explicit guide to make canning foods in your home an accurate, practical and SAFE process.

LOUISE W. HAMILTON, R.D.
Professor of Foods and Nutrition

GERALD D. KUHN, Ph.D.
Associate Professor, Food Science

KAREN A. RUGH
Communications Specialist

THE PENNSYLVANIA STATE UNIVERSITY
Cooperative Extension Service

CHAPTER I

Benefits
of Home Canning

It's like getting "A's" on your report card, when you hear the *pings* that tell you your canning jars are sealing. And that's only today's reward. As you label sparkling jars of fruits, vegetables and meats and put them away in a "cool dark place," you can hardly help gloating over them, relishing the months ahead. What pleasure to go into your own pantry or fruit cellar for quality home canned food to feed your family, to serve to privileged guests or to carry proudly to a friend.

While it is no longer necessary—as it once was—for each family to preserve summer's harvest for winter eating, people continue to can for reasons of their own. In fact, canning is gaining in popularity as a whole new generation experience the pleasures of gardening and preserving.

Whether you thriftily can everything in your garden, or put up only a few specialties you couldn't buy— such as prize pickles and relishes—you probably think about such benefits as these:

Nutritional quality

If you have access to fresh-picked garden produce from your own garden, your neighbor's garden, a farm stand, farmers' market, or one of the new "pick-your-own" farms . . . and if you get this food into canning jars within a few hours after picking . . . you have an enormous advantage over someone who buys "fresh" food at the store. The nutritional value of canned garden-fresh vegetables is often equal to or better than freshly cooked vegetables that have lingered in the supermarket. Thus, your home-canned foods can help you serve more nutritious, better balanced meals throughout the year.

The main sources of vitamins A and C in our diets are fruits and vegetables. If you eat them when they're ripe and fresh-picked, you get full measure of important nutrients.

But once picked, they begin to lose vitamins . . . some slowly, some quite rapidly. Properly stored, in a cold cellar or equivalent, apples, carrots, potatoes or winter squash retain freshness and thus, vitamins. But such highly perishable foods as berries, sweet corn and peas wilt fast. And vitamins depart with the freshness.

Ideally, foods to be canned should be of a suitable variety; harvested at peak maturity or ripened after picking, if necessary; prepared and heat sterilized according to recommended directions, and stored under proper conditions. Following these good procedures, it's possible to retain from 60 to 70 percent of vitamin C (ascorbic acid), nearly one half of the B-vitamin thiamin, and virtually all of vitamin A. If foods are stored in a cool (45°F, 7°C), dry, dark place for a year, there should be almost no nutrient loss or quality change. Note, however, that canned food stored at 85°F (30°C) for a year will lose an additional 30 percent of vitamin C and thiamin content.

When you open your home canned food, follow these guidelines to insure maximum nutritional benefit:
• Heat foods rapidly in a small amount of liquid. Never allow foods to soak for a long period of time.
• Use the liquids from canned foods. Vegetable juices make good sauces and gravies. Liquid from canned fruit may be used in gelatin salads or, if appropriate, in a beverage.
• Store open jars of food, covered, in the refrigerator.
• Serve foods attractively to stimulate appetites. Food not eaten wastes valuable nutrients and money.

Restricted diets

If someone in your family is on a low-sugar or low-sodium diet, you can put up foods to follow doctor's orders, perhaps canning in smaller jars for convenience. Pint and half-pint jars are ideal for small families, too.

Conservation and Ecology

Most home canners are influenced by an eleventh commandment: "Thou shalt not waste." During the growing season, the supply of fresh food at peak condition is generally more than a gardener's family can eat or give away. It would be sinful to waste it . . . so out come the canning jars!

The leftovers from canning—skins and cores—can enrich your compost pile and later be returned to the garden soil. And in a sense, canning equipment is also recycled. In good condition, standard canning jars last for years; screw bands, if not dented or rusted, can be used many times. (The lids, of course, cannot be reused and must be replaced each season.) Major canning equipment is usually a one-time investment.

The economics of canning

Canning is the most economical of all methods of preserving food at home. (Only sun drying in dry climates—free energy—is cheaper.) But whether it proves so for you will depend on a number of variables: cost of produce (was it a gift?), quality and kind of produce (how much do you have to trim or throw away?), method of heat sterilization, kind of equipment and amount of food canned at a given time. You should also figure cost of labor, energy (gas or electricity), water and any added ingredients such as sugar and vinegar.

Food costs

Enthusiastic first-year gardeners, astonished by the yields from even a small plot, are tempted to think of their harvest as "free food." But of course it isn't. Home gardeners must reckon costs of seed or bedding plants, tilling, fertilizer, garden tools, pesticides, water and perhaps rental fee for the garden plot. Also, even experienced gardeners suffer some crop failures. But still, growing your own produce is normally more economical than buying fresh produce for canning. In addition, some gardeners value the physical exercise, family participation, convenience and pride as part of the payoff.

Labor costs

In purely economic terms, if you have marketable skills, you may be able to earn more dollars working than you can save by growing and canning your own food. Most research on home canning shows the greatest savings when the produce is home-grown, and when jars and equipment costs are spread over years of use. After that, it's up to you if you want to put a dollar evaluation on your gardening/canning hours, to figure whether home preserving is "profitable."

If gardening is recreation for you . . . if the idea of doing for yourself—independence—is important in your family philosophy . . . if you take real pleasure in the work, real pride in the results . . . the payoff may be far greater in real satisfactions than the monetary value. Only you can decide.

Equipment costs

Canning jars, screw bands and lids will amount to a sizable initial investment only if you start canning in a big way. Cost of one dozen new canning units (jars, screw bands and lids) will range from $2.30 to $3.50. (All prices quoted here are 1976 prices.) Canning jars and screw bands should last ten years—maybe longer for jars. Recommended lids cost from three to eight cents each and are NOT recommended for re-use, regardless of manufacturer's claims.

Boiling water canners range in price from $8 to $15. And the other small equipment recommended for home canning varies considerably in price; some of it you may have on hand.

If you limit your canning to fruits and pickles, you can get along with the boiling water canner. But if you plan to can vegetables and meats, you must invest in a pressure canner, or borrow one. (Some new pressure saucepans are also suitable for home canning.)

Commonly used models of pressure canners range in price from $40 to $75. Although the initial expense is considerable, the life expectancy of a pressure canner, properly cared for, is 15 years or longer. However, expect to buy some replacement parts after a few years: a new gasket, or on some models, a new pressure gauge.

How much food should you can?

Home canning proves wasteful when you preserve foods your family won't eat, or when you can more than you will use within one year.* Until you've had some experience, it's not easy to calculate how much garden to plant, or how much produce to buy for canning.

If you keep a canning diary from year to year, you will soon have a useful file of information. This diary should include an inventory list of everything you canned this year: variety of fruit or vegetable if you know it, size jar, number of jars, recipe name and source, date canned, storage or shelf location. As you eat the food, add notes about its quality—will you want to can this variety or this recipe again? And quantity—did you can enough to get you through the winter? The inventory will help you know what you have on hand, and will help you rotate your stock—so you use up older jars first.

It's also useful to make diary notes about heat sterilizing times and tips on using equipment that you might forget from one year to the next. Especially valuable will be notes on how much food (pounds, bushels, or garden rows) it takes to fill X-number jars.

Another way to estimate how much food to can in summer for winter eating, is to think about your family's nutritional needs. Each person needs to eat at least four fruits and/or vegetables daily. Each day, we need one that's rich in vitamin C; every other day, we need a good source of vitamin A.

How many times a week might you serve a particular fruit or vegetable? How often would you serve it canned (as opposed to fresh or frozen)? Will one quart jar serve your family? If you calculate the number of jars you need of each food, each week, and multiply it by the number of weeks you'll be eating from jars rather than from the garden, you have some indication of the number of jars to be filled. Tables in Chapter V (fruits) and VI (vegetables) tell you how much fresh food it takes to fill quart jars.

---

*Under excellent storage conditions, canned foods will keep longer than one year. But few homes today have the "cool, dry, dark place" that insures keeping quality. Therefore, it's best to can only as much as you will eat before next year's crop is harvested.

CHAPTER II

How to Be Sure Your Home Canned Food Is Safe

Old cookbooks make interesting reading, but they don't always contain information and directions that apply today. We can afford to be nostalgic about some things from "the good old days," but not about old, unsafe methods of canning.

Despite grandmother's professed success with canning foods, it is now known that some of her methods and equipment did not always result in safe canned foods.

The fact that unsafe canning is still a problem today is almost unthinkable—it is not for lack of knowledge. Scientific research completed between 1920 and 1930 on canning provided absolute controls which remain accurate after more than 45 years of use. So the problem has always been—and continues to be—errors in using what we know.

Almost every canning book published before 1955 gives some directions that are in error. Even some canning directions printed in the 1970s are in error and if used would result in potentially unsafe canned food. It's a fact that most spoilage and outbreaks of botulism are caused by use of procedures and methods known for more than 45 years to be unsafe, or by use of improper or faulty canning equipment.

Why do people take chances? Many home canners have been slow and/or remarkably casual about adopting safe procedures. In some cases, it's simple lack of knowledge. Maybe the person who taught unsafe methods didn't fully understand the proper methods and gave faulty directions. Sometimes a recipe is in error.

Sometimes it's a matter of someone cutting corners to save time or money. If you're tired or under pressure to finish the job, you may take a shortcut in the sublime belief that if grandma always did it so and nobody apparently suffered food poisoning, it will be okay this time, too.

The purpose of this book is to help all home canners—experienced "old hands" as well as beginners— better understand the *reasons* for the recommended methods. Computers may blindly follow any directions they're programmed for— but people usually don't want to do anything unless they understand *why*. If you learn what causes spoilage in the first place, then it's easy to remember what you must do to prevent it, so that food you preserve will be of top quality and safe to eat.

Rest assured: Foods canned at home *can* and *should* be safe! Control of all microorganisms capable of causing spoilage in canned food, and especially spoilage resulting in botulism, is *not* a hit-or-miss practice.

SAFE CANNING DEFINED

Spoilage in canned foods is caused by molds, yeasts and bacteria, collectively called microorganisms. They grow best in moist, warm food, in the presence and some in the absence of air. In fact, air itself is a spoiler: not only does it contain microorganisms that can contaminate food, air also oxidizes* food—makes it turn dark.

If food is to be safely canned, all living forms of these microorganisms (spoilers) must be destroyed and air must be kept out to avoid recontamination. This is done by heat sterilization: by heating the food in the jar, with lid in place, to the degree necessary to kill microorganisms contained in or on the food or the jar. In the process, the steam of heat sterilization exhausts the air from the jar. Then, as the jar

---

*Oxidation is covered in Chapter IV. It's a chemical reaction of air with food and is stopped by blanching, or by treating fresh-cut foods with an antioxidant, or by removing air.

cools, the lid makes a vacuum seal which prevents the re-entry of any new spoilers or air which could recontaminate or otherwise lower the quality of the food.

The degree of heat you need to kill microorganisms depends on the food you are sterilizing . . . whether it is *acid food* or *low-acid food*.

Acid foods, if sterilized for an adequate length of time, may be safely canned in a boiling water canner. But low-acid foods must be sterilized at a higher temperature—in a pressure canner.

Most foods contain various types of acid. The amounts and kinds are easily measured in the laboratory and scientists have told us which foods are acid foods and which are low in acid.

Modern directions for canning—how long to heat sterilize individual foods, for example, and whether or not to use a pressure canner—are based on the acid level in foods plus other scientific findings. Such modern directions—*if scrupulously followed*—virtually eliminate any kind of spoilage in foods canned at home.

WHAT YOU SHOULD KNOW ABOUT BOTULISM

Botulism is an illness caused by eating foods which contain a potent neuro-toxin produced by bacteria called *Clostridium botulinum*. While absolute controls for preventing botulism in canned food have been identified and available since before 1930, botulism traceable to eating home canned foods resulted in more than 700 deaths in the United States between 1930 and 1975. Even with modern medical diagnosis and treatment, botulism causes an average of four or five deaths each year, and is fatal to about one fourth of the people who eat affected foods.

Clostridium botulinum exists in either of two living forms, depending on its environment. The active or reproductive form is called a "vegetative cell." The inactive or dormant form is called a "spore."

Spores are contained in all soils and in some lake and sea water, and are, therefore, also found on the surface of most plant and animal food sources consumed by humans. But neither spores nor vegetative cells alone are harmful. In fact, every day people eat these bacteria without ill effects.

In some ways, bacterial spores are like plant seeds. Seeds can survive winter and droughts, waiting for good growing conditions before they sprout. Spores, too, can survive in dormant form until conditions are right for germinating and forming new vegetative cells. Within a few days in an ideal environment (such as in a jar of canned food), the vegetative cells reproduce to astronomical numbers. As they become overpopulated and begin to die, they produce the neuro-toxin responsible for botulism, along with a new crop of spores. If you eat food containing the toxin, you will develop botulism.

Cleanliness—even vigorous scrubbing of fresh foods—is not enough to remove all bacterial spores before food goes into the canning jars. Thus, remaining bacteria must be destroyed inside the canning jar—by heat sterilization. If temperatures and sterilizing times are not high enough or long enough to kill these heat-resistant bacteria, the surviving spores may find conditions inside the jar ideal for growth.

To survive and grow, bacterial vegetative cells require all the following conditions:
- moist, low-acid food, such as vegetables, fish, and other seafood, milk or any animal meat.
- a suitable temperature of from 40° to 120°F (5° to 49°C); growing best between 86° and 95°F (30° to 35°C).
- a low-oxygen environment, such as provided by tightly sealed vacuum-packaged or canned food.

You can see that botulism is not a worry with any fresh food still out in the air, nor with any refrigerated or frozen food (too cold for the growth of the vegetative cells), nor with properly dried food (not enough moisture).

Nor is it likely to develop in any acid food . . . the vegetative cells of *Clostridium botulinum* grow only on low-acid foods.*

Cautionary note: If the heat sterilization period is not long enough to kill *all* types of heat-resistant bacteria in acid foods, it is possible that some other kinds of bacteria will grow inside the sealed jar. Such growth may lead to mold growth. Certain types of mold growth lower the acidity in food. Thus, an acid food could turn into a low-acid food inside the jar—setting up ideal conditions for the germination of *Clostridium botulinum*. This is why it is important to follow heat sterilization schedules for acid foods, especially tomatoes, as recommended in Chapter V.

ACID CLASSIFICATION OF CANNED FOODS

The quantity of acid in canned food is best expressed as a "pH" value. The values of pH range from 0 to 14. A value of 7 indicates that food is neutral, being neither acid nor alka-line. As food is increasingly more alkaline, the pH value increases from 7 to 14. As food is increasingly more acid, the pH value decreases from 7 to 0. Most foods have a pH value somewhere between 3.0 and 8.0.

Clostridum botulinum will not grow in foods with a pH of 4.5 or lower, *but will grow* in foods having a pH of 4.6 or higher. Therefore, as used in canning terminology, foods having a pH of 4.5 or lower are called "acid foods." These are easily and safely heat sterilized in a boiling water canner.

Foods having a pH of 4.6 or higher are called "low-acid foods." (If you're not a chemist, it's a little hard to remember this because it's backward: a *high* pH means *low* acid.) Low-acid foods include all meat, poultry, seafoods, soups, milk, and all fresh vegetables except tomatoes. Low-acid foods support the growth of *Clostridium botulinum* and other heat-resistant bacteria capable of causing spoilage in canned foods. To be safely canned, they need to be heat sterilized at temperatures higher than boiling water—that is, in a pressure canner.

Types of acid foods

Acid foods are acid because they grow that way, or because acids form when the food is fermented, or because acid (vinegar) is added when pickling.

Some examples of foods containing natural acids at harvest (enough acid to have a pH value of 4.5 or lower) are: fruits, including apricots, apples, cherries, peaches, pears, plums, all types of berries, and tomatoes. All these foods can be safely heat sterilized in a boiling water canner.

Sauerkraut and other properly fermented vegetables are acid foods because, during fermentation, their natural sugars are converted to natural acids by bacterial action. They, too, can be safely heat sterilized in a boiling water canner. *But* if the cabbage and other vegetables were *im*properly fermented, the result may be spoilage or formation of too little acid. Such a product would not be safe for canning in a boiling water canner.

Some of the reasons why fermenting vegetables may not form enough acid:

- Vegetables not fresh, or not properly handled.
- Vegetables have too little natural sugar.
- Not enough salt in the brine.
- Too high or too low fermenting temperature.
- Uncontrolled mold growth on the liquid surface of fermenting vegetables.

Vegetables pickled with vinegar are also classified as acid foods—providing they're properly prepared and controlled. The vinegar used should be labeled "5 percent acid strength" or "5 percent acidity" (50 grains). A bottle labeled 4 percent is not strong enough.

Do NOT use homemade vinegar; often it contains too little acetic acid to be used safely in published recipes for pickling cucumbers, beets and other vegetables.

In pickling, as in fermenting, molds also present a problem. Uncontrolled mold growth on the liquid surface of vegetables while pickling, may reduce the acidity of the product. The result would be not only an obviously spoiled product, but also a low-acid product unsafe for heat sterilization in a boiling water canner.

HEAT STERILIZING: RECOMMENDED METHODS

The *boiling water canner* may be used to heat sterilize all acid foods (pH of 4.5 or lower). They are:

Apples	Pears
Applesauce	Pickles
Apricots	Pineapple
Berries	Plums
Cherries	Rhubarb
Fruit butters	Sauerkraut
Fruit juices	Tomatoes
Fruit purees	Tomato juice
Jams, jellies, preserves	Tomato sauce or puree
Peaches	without meat

In Chapter V, you will find step-by-step directions for preparing, packing and sterilizing acid foods.

Use the *pressure canner* to heat sterilize all low-acid foods (pH of 4.6 or higher). If you do not have a pressure canner, do not can these foods:

Vegetables

Asparagus	Mushrooms
Beans, lima	Peas
Beans, snap,	Potatoes
green or wax	Pumpkin
Beets	Soup
Carrots	Spinach
Corn, whole kernel	Squash, summer
Corn, cream style	and winter

Meat and poultry
   Tomato sauce with meat
   Chicken or rabbit
   Chopped meat
   Meat strips or cubes
   Sausage

In Chapter VI you will find step-by-step directions for preparing, packing and sterilizing low-acid foods.

Sterilization schedules

The *length of time* it takes to heat sterilize foods—whether in boiling water canner or pressure canner—depends on the kind of food and the size of the jar.

Heat penetrates more slowly in starchy foods such as corn, lima beans and peas; in solid foods such as pumpkin; and in foods that pack closely together such as spinach or other leafy vegetables. Such foods require longer sterilizing times than beets or green beans, for example, because it takes longer for heat to reach a high enough temperature for a long enough time to sterilize food in the center of the jar.

These requirements are reflected in the heat sterilization times given for both quart and pint jars of each individual fruit, vegetable and meat (see Chapters V and VI).

OTHER SPOILAGE AGENTS

Any growth of bacteria, yeast or mold in canned food will result in spoilage. It can develop in any food that was not sterilized properly, or in jars that fail to seal after cooling and become recontaminated with air-borne microorganisms.

The growth of certain molds on some foods produces substances known as *mycotoxins*. Some mycotoxins are harmful. Any canned foods, including jams, jellies and preserves, having obvious signs of mold growth *should not be eaten*. The entire contents of affected jars should be discarded. Skimming off surface mold may not remove all mycotoxins present in the food.

Because certain mold growth may be harmful, and because growth of *Clostridium botulinum* is always harmful—often fatal—DO NOT EAT OR TASTE ANY SPOILED FOOD.

Detecting spoilage

The most obvious sign of spoilage in home canned food is a swollen lid or liquid leaking from the jar. Any swelling of jar lids signals potential hazards. *Do not taste or serve food from such a jar.* The swelling is the result of gases produced by growth of microorganisms. The condition known as "working" or "fermenting" is the rapid production of gas by some spoilage yeasts and bacteria, with visible symptoms of gas bubbles rising to the surface of the food in the jar.

You can also detect spoilage of canned food by unusual or abnormal food colors, such as: a cloudy or darkened color in liquid or brine in canned vegetables and meats; a visible white or colored film on the top surface of food; or a cotton-like mold growth of several possible colors on the surface of food. *Do not taste or serve any part of foods having these spoilage symptoms.* Discard entire contents of jar.

Not all food spoilage is signaled by a swollen lid or abnormal color. Jars with normal concave lids and without any other visible symptoms of spoilage may, when opened, give off noticeable abnormal food odors. These odors may be described as yeasty, moldy, sour or putrid. Again, these are definite symptoms of spoilage. *Do not taste or serve food from such a jar.*

Some spoilage microorganisms grow without producing gases; still others produce soluble gases. Thus, jars spoiled by these microorganisms will have vacuum seals and normal-appearing concave dome lids. An example of this kind of spoilage is known as "flat-sour." It is not detectable except for an unpleasant sourish flavor. While harmless, most people would refuse to eat such food.

There is a special class of potential spoilage bacteria known as *thermophiles*, meaning they love heat. In fact, they grow only at temperatures above 95°F (35°C). Spoilage is easy to prevent by cooling jars of canned food to 70°F to 80°F (21°C to 27°C) and storing them below 85°F (30°C).

Neither commercial nor home canning procedures kill all thermophilic spores. The quantity of heat needed to kill them would ruin the food by reducing flavor, color, texture and nutrients to an unacceptable level; but spoilage by these bacteria is always harmless.

OTHER UNSAFE CANNING PRACTICES

A few canning practices—part of the folklore of canning—have never been safe, and we want to warn against them here.

Open kettle canning is no longer recommended—not even for jams and preserves. Open kettle canning means the food is cooked in an open kettle, packed boiling hot in sterilized jars and quickly sealed, with no heat treatment after the food is packed in the jars. This is an unsafe practice which has resulted in food spoilage and even botulism. Heating foods to boiling in an open kettle is not enough to destroy spoilage organisms that may be in food. And it is impossible to prevent spoilage microorganisms in air from recontaminating foods while ladling or pouring them from kettle to jar. Also, there may be contamination in jars and lids.

Although many women still do it, sealing jams and jellies with paraffin is also not a safe practice. The natural acidity in fruit, plus sugar, helps preserve these foods, but does not prevent molds from developing—and we are just beginning to recognize the hazards to humans and animals from eating mycotoxins produced by molds.

Since microwave ovens have become more wide-spread, the idea of oven canning has come up again. Unfortunately, the use-and-care booklets that came with some early models of microwave ovens gave directions for oven canning. Such directions have since been retracted. So keep this rule in mind: *NEVER try to can anything in any kind of oven— conventional or microwave.* It is a dangerous practice. Here's why:

When food-filled jars are placed in boiling water or pressure canners, the balance of pressure inside and outside the jars is equalized throughout the heat sterilizing process. But in the dry heat of the oven, glass jars may not tolerate the unbalanced high internal pressure—and an explosion may result. Equally important, heat distribution in an oven is uneven so the center of some jars may never reach the sterilizing point. Also, lids may not seal properly in the dry heat of an oven. Finally, metal (in the jar lids) should not be used in microwave ovens.

Unbelievable as it seems, we have heard that some home canners have tried to use the dishwasher for processing food in jars. The typical temperature of water in a dishwasher is 130° to 160°F (55° to 70°C)—not nearly hot enough to sterilize food. *NEVER use a dishwasher to process canned food.*

Another unsafe practice is canning with aspirin. Aspirin does not contain enough acid to change the acidity or pH value of food being canned. Therefore, aspirin cannot replace or reduce the heat sterilization needed to can food safely; it is not a preservative.

The term *cold pack* is confusing; it is not a canning method. It refers only to temperature of food packed in jars. All jars filled with unheated food must be sterilized in either boiling water or pressure canners.

See Chapter VII for a summary of errors that can cause spoilage in home-canned foods, along with directions for checking on its safety.

CHAPTER III

Canning Equipment

Whether you are shopping for the first time for canning equipment, or checking over your equipment before the canning season starts, information in this chapter will help you. After the descriptions of the canners, jars and lids, you will find information on maintenance and storage. There's also a discussion of new jar lids appearing on the market.

BOILING WATER CANNER

Boiling Water Canner
Description: A boiling water canner is a deep kettle fitted with a tight cover and a rack to hold jars. The rack keeps jars

evenly spaced and off the bottom of the canner, out of direct contact with heat, so they won't crack. This also helps distribute heat evenly during sterilization. (Replacement racks may be available where canning supplies are sold, or from manufacturers.)

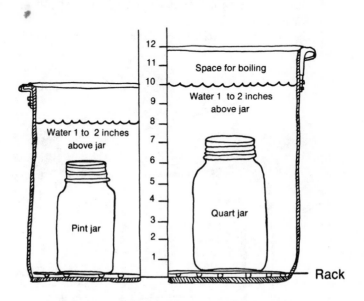

BOILING WATER LEVELS

Selection: Most boiling water canners are either aluminum or porcelain-enamel. There's little difference in price; you should choose the canner best suited to your range. If you cook with gas, a canner with a ridged bottom will be more economical to use because the heating surface is increased. Smooth, flat-bottomed canners make better heat contact with electric units.

To insure that all jars will be adequately heat sterilized, the diameter of the canner should be no more than 4 inches greater than the burner on which you intend to use it.

Canner should be at least 10 inches tall for quarts and 7 inches tall for pints. This allows at least one inch, but preferably two inches, of rapidly boiling water to cover jars of food placed on the rack. A canner deep enough to hold quart jars can, of course, be used for pints. A good fitting lid on your canner keeps water actively boiling with a minimum of energy, and limits evaporation.

You can improvise a boiling water canner if you have a kettle that is deep enough, has a rack and lid, and fits on the burner. But do not use larger or oval-shaped containers that fit over two burners. The jars between burners, or around the edge of a container that's too big, will not get enough heat for proper sterilization.

Directions for using boiling water canner in Chapter V.

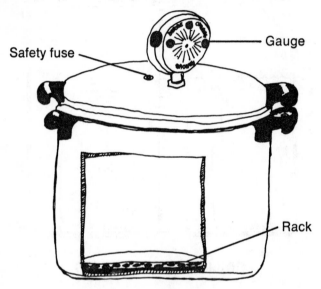

Safety fuse

Gauge

Rack

PRESSURE CANNER

Pressure Canner

If you plan to can low-acid foods, a pressure canner is an essential piece of equipment.

Pressure canners are safe to use. But some homemakers are reluctant to use them because they've heard tales of explosions. The design problem responsible for explosions was corrected many decades ago. Now, by regulation, all pressure canners are equipped with either a safety valve or fuse—a mechanical device that simply blows out when pressure becomes too great.

Description: A pressure canner is a deep heavy kettle—most are cast aluminum—fitted with a rack to keep jars evenly spaced and off the bottom of the canner. (Jars may break if they're in direct contact with bottom of kettle or burner.) Around the edge of the tight-fitting lid, there is a channel for a rubber gasket. When the lid is locked in place, steam pressure builds up inside the canner, pushing against the gasket and sealing the canner.

There are two general types of pressure canners. One has a dial gauge that indicates pressure inside the canner. The other has a calibrated or weighted gauge that actually controls the pressure.

Both types of canners have an air vent to allow all the air inside the canner to escape during exhausting; then the vent is closed so that steam pressure can build up.

The vent on older dial gauge models is called a petcock—a type of valve which is manually opened or closed. The vent on newer dial gauge canners is closed by putting a weight over it.

Because of their potential inaccuracy, dial gauge models require regular maintenance (information follows). And while using canner, you must read the dial frequently and regulate heat if necessary to avoid uneven pressure that would result in inadequate heat sterilization.

On pressure canners with a weighted gauge, the gauge itself is used to close the vent once the air is exhausted. Also, the weighted gauge releases any excess pressure during the sterilization process—an additional safety feature. While some people are bothered by the sound of a jiggling weighted gauge, others consider it an advantage as it signals proper heat control during the entire heat sterilization time without a visual check.

Selection: Pressure canners vary in size and capacity. The smallest size available holds four quart or seven pint jars. For a family interested in canning only small quantities of low-acid foods, it would be perfectly adequate.

The most popular pressure canner is medium-size, holding 7 quart or 10 pint jars. The large canners hold 7 quarts or 20 pints arranged in two layers. But these large canners require ample clearance between range surface and hood and when fully loaded are difficult for one person to lift. They also require longer exhaust time.

Pressure saucepans, while not generally recommended, may be used to heat sterilize pints or half-pints, if pressure can be maintained at 10 pounds, and 20 minutes are added to heat sterilization time. This extra time is necessary because the lighter weight construction of the saucepan permits more rapid heating and cooling.

Maintenance of pressure canners

A dial gauge canner should be checked for accuracy each year—dial gauges do get out of adjustment. You can get it checked at "clinics" offered by some county Cooperative Extension Service offices, or at stores where canning equipment is sold.

Or you may check your own dial gauge with a maximum thermometer. When gauge reads 5 pounds, maximum thermometer should read 228°F (109°C); 10 pounds, 240°F (115°C); and 15 pounds, 250°F (121°C). Higher or lower temperatures indicate inaccuracies in gauge; a lower temperature (off 2°F or 1°C or more) signals need for gauge replacement.

MAXIMUM THERMOMETER

A maximum thermometer works like an ordinary fever thermometer. You put it in an empty jar and put it through a 5-minute test inside the canner at the pressure you are checking. It records the highest temperature achieved and you can read this when you open the canner. Before use, thermometer should be shaken down to 220°F (105°C) or below. Maximum thermometers may be available from local sources, or from Taylor Instrument Company, Rochester, New York, 14602. Model numbers 21464-1 (nylon casing) and 21464-2 (steel casing) are recommended. Price of maximum thermometers ranges from $12 to $18.

Weighted gauges do not get out of adjustment and do not need to be checked for accuracy. But they do need to be kept clean. Wash carefully in clean, sudsy water after each use—do not let residue dry on. If you can't remove food particles by washing, use a toothpick to clean gauge openings—do not use a metal pick which may scratch the gauge. Rinse gauge thoroughly, dry and store in a dry place to avoid any possible corrosion. Also check the gasket. If your canner cannot maintain pressure, it's a signal that the gasket is not properly seated or that you need to replace the gasket.

Directions for using pressure canner in Chapter VI.

Ranges

Early models of some ceramic smooth-top electric ranges may not generate enough heat to maintain a vigorous boil or proper pressure in your canner. If you own such a range, test your equipment on it before you try to use it to heat sterilize foods. Some ranges with a second oven at eye level may not have clearance for a big canner.

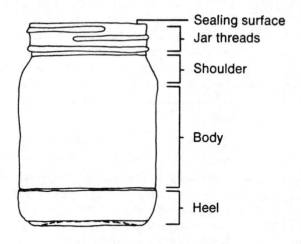

Sealing surface
Jar threads
Shoulder
Body
Heel

STANDARD MASON JAR

Jars

The standard Mason* jar is a wide-mouth glass jar with a screw top made especially for home canning. It is fully tempered to withstand heat sterilizing temperatures and the top

---

* named for John L. Mason, a New Yorker who took out patents in 1858 for improvements in screw-top glass jars.

sealing edge is of uniform thickness so the lid will seal properly. Several manufacturers offer Mason jars under their own brand names, in half-pint, pint, pint-and-a-half and quart sizes.

Some commercial products are marketed in standard canning jars and are so labeled. These are reusable for home canning. But most jars used to pack commercially-made products such as mayonnaise, pickles and coffee, are not recommended for home canning. The sealing edge of such "one-trip" jars may not be uniform or wide enough and, therefore, may not seal properly. Also, the neck of the jar may not be deep enough so screw band holds lid firmly in place.

It's especially important to use standard canning jars for meats and vegetables that must be heat sterilized in a pressure canner. The initial cost of jars is well worth the price. With careful handling, proper cleaning and storage, your jars should last a long time.

If they're in good condition, free of cloudy or scaly deposits, used canning jars may be a wise buy—if the price is right. A reliable guide to quality is the manufacturer's name on the jar. But compare the price of used jars with that of new jars of similar size. Antique jars are not recommended; they were made for shoulder sealing with rubber rings, and the top edge may not be smooth and even enough to use two-piece metal lids.

Before-season check: All jars, new or used, must be free of cracks and chips, especially on the sealing surface which, for most lids, is the top rim of the jar. Look carefully at the top of each jar by holding it at eye level. If you wear glasses for close work, make sure you wear them for this test. If there is a chip or nick, a bump, depression, or hairline crack on sealing surface, lid may not seal properly or jars may break during heat sterilization.

Make sure there are no cloudy-appearing scales or deposits on the inside of jars. Spores of bacteria under these scales are difficult to remove. Fill affected jar with full strength vinegar and allow to stand for two to three hours. Re-use vinegar in same way to clean other jars having cloudy deposits. Then scrub inside of jars with a stiff brush or a non-abrasive scouring pad such as nylon net or plastic.

Jar Lids

The 2-piece metal lids made by established firms have a long record of safe use based on years of experience by home canners. The lid itself is flat, enameled on the underside to keep food from reacting with the metal; it has a rubber sealing compound around the edge. The metal screw band holds the lid in place during the heat sterilization and cooling periods. As jars are heated, any air inside the jar is forced out by steam—there's enough "give" in the 2-piece lid for air to escape. As jars cool, a vacuum is created, making a hermetic seal; you can hear the *ping* as the rubber-edged lid seals itself to the top of the jar. And when you look at it, the lid will be obviously concave—pulled down by the vacuum inside the jar.

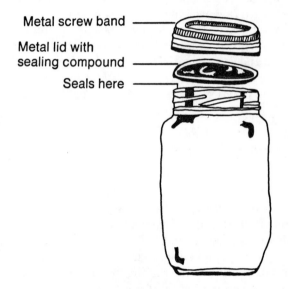

Metal screw band

Metal lid with sealing compound

Seals here

TWO-PIECE LID

Buy the number of new and replacement lids you'll need early in the canning season. Supplies may be limited. Shopping early will also give you time to compare prices and get the best buys. Use the information in Chapter I to estimate the number of jars you'll can and number of jar lids you'll need. Think about the best jar sizes for various foods—to avoid long refrigerator storage of opened jars.

In response to the shortage of the 2-piece metal lids recommended for home canning, numerous new jar lids are appearing on the market. At this writing, the lids are so new there has not been enough time for researchers or home canners to evaluate their effectiveness in maintaining proper seals for the expected shelf life of home canned foods.

Early experience shows that some new lids do not consistently seal and/or maintain a seal. Some 2- and 3-piece lids cannot have the screw band removed without losing the vacuum seal; nor can 1-piece lids be removed. This prevents the removal of food residue from jar threads after sterilizing, thereby increasing the possibility of recontamination of foods during storage. Such lids may also rust and be difficult to remove if jars are stored in damp areas. (This is more of a problem with raw pack than hot pack food.)

If trying one of the many new brands of canning lids on the market, buy only a small quantity at first; make sure you like them and can get satisfactory seals using them. Be especially careful about overfilling jars and wiping sealing surfaces—bad practices increase the risk of lid failure.

Always save and follow manufacturer's instructions for preparing lids and adjusting for tightness—directions differ from brand to brand.

Before-season check: Inspect all lids for defects before use. Examine both stored and new lids to see if they are free of gaps in sealing compound. Also check pliability of sealing compound—it should spring back when pressed gently with fingernail. Check lids for rusting or scratches in enamel. Do not use less than perfect lids for heat sterilizing.

Screw bands are reusable if not rusted during storage, or dented or bent from being pried loose. Most standard screw bands can be used on various makes of standard canning jars. It is advisable to check to be sure screw bands fit snugly before you begin canning. If you're not sure, use screw bands that are the same brand as your canning jars. Screw bands that do not fit jars and lids correctly fail to apply adequate tension on lids and may result in unsealed jars.

Other jar closures

Also in use, but not as safe or easy to use, are porcelain-lined zinc caps with a separate rubber ring. If you are using this type of jar closure, jar rings must be *new* jar rings. They should never be re-used.

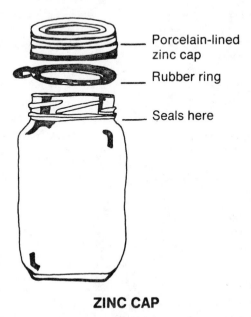

Porcelain-lined zinc cap

Rubber ring

Seals here

ZINC CAP

Before heat sterilizing filled jars, the caps are screwed tight against the rubber ring, then loosened ¼ inch to permit air to escape during sterilization. Caps must be retightened when jars are removed from canner to make the seal. Also, you can see that the separate rubber ring must seal to both jar and cap—doubling the risk of a seal failure.

The jars called "lightning jars" with glass lids and wire bails also employ separate rubber rings to make the seal. Moreover, the wire bails must have enough tension to seal rubber to glass. Because they weaken with age, this is a serious shortcoming.

Finally, it is not possible to determine if you have a perfect seal with either the zinc or glass caps—there is no test as there is with 2-piece lids. You can only check for leakage.

If you have jars and lids of this type, the best advice is to use them for refrigerator preserves. We do not recommend them for heat sterilizing.

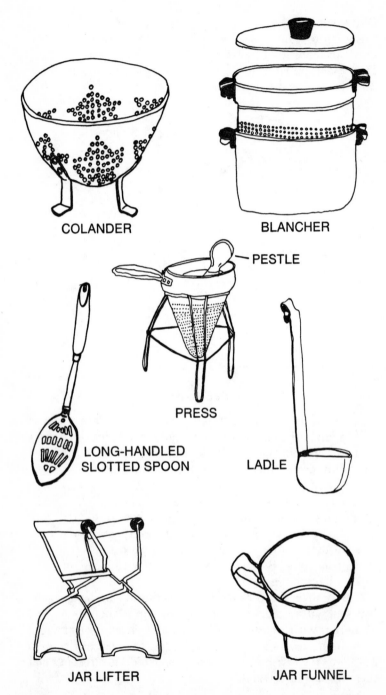

COLANDER

BLANCHER

PESTLE

PRESS

LONG-HANDLED
SLOTTED SPOON

LADLE

JAR LIFTER

JAR FUNNEL

Small equipment

Some of the tools described here are especially made for canning—others are ordinary kitchen tools which are useful.

Colander (or large sieve)
Useful to lift fruits and vegetables out of water.

Blancher
A perforated basket that fits inside a flat-bottom large pot. Foods placed in the basket are easily and safely lowered into boiling water, transferred to cold water and removed from cold water to drain. Use it for blanching, for wilting leafy vegetables and for scalding and cooling tomatoes and peaches to remove skins.

Press
A perforated metal cone fitted with a wooden pestle. Size of holes allows juice to pass through, but not stems, skins, cores or seeds. Rotate the pestle to press juice from heated fruits and tomatoes.

Long-handled slotted spoon
Useful for stirring cooking foods in large kettles and for putting pieces of hot cooked food into canning jars.

Ladle
Useful for filling jars with liquid.

Jar funnel
Extremely useful—it helps keep food and liquid off the top edge of the jar when you're filling it; also reduces spillage.

Jar lifter
Essential to remove hot jars from boiling water or pressure canner safely without touching jars.

Storing equipment

Pressure canner. Because a pressure canner is a major investment, you will want to take good care of it so it will provide years of service. Do not submerge the lid of a dial gauge canner in water, but wash it well inside and out with hot sudsy water. The lid of a weighted gauge canner may be immersed, but be careful to use clean dishwater so no particles of food can be trapped in the vent or under the gasket. Keep all grease from gasket. Make sure food and corrosion don't build up inside vent or weight. Rinse and dry the lid well. Wash and rinse the canner and rack. When all parts are completely dry, store the lid upside down in the canner. At the end of canning season, place crumpled newspaper inside the canner to absorb any moisture. Store in a dry place.

Boiling water canner. Wash boiling water canner, lid and rack in hot sudsy water and rinse well. When thoroughly dry, store the lid upside down in the canner. At the end of the season, place crumpled newspapers inside canner to absorb any moisture. Store in a dry place.

Screw bands. Wash screw bands in hot sudsy water, rinse and dry thoroughly. Because some have a tendency to rust, store them in a dry place. Do not store in a plastic bag; instead, put them in a mesh bag or open box, or thread them on string or wire so air can get to them. Lids, of course, should be discarded after one use.

Jars. As you use canned foods, wash empty jars in a dishwasher or by hand. If possible, store them in original cartons, covered but not capped.

CHAPTER IV

General Directions for Home Canning

Creative cooking should be encouraged—but not in home canning! There is no room here for improvising or inventing new methods. Proven scientific procedures must be followed to the letter and to the minute if you want spoilage-free, high quality food. This chapter covers:
- Canning salt
- Methods of packing jars (hot pack, raw pack)
- Overall work plan
- Preparing jars and lids (sterilizing, etc.)
- Selecting foods for canning
- Washing fruits and vegetables
- Treating to prevent darkening
- Sugar, artificial sweeteners and sugar syrup
- Preventing fruit from floating in jars
- Filling jars
- Importance of head space
- Releasing air bubbles
- Closing jars
- Heat sterilizing (refer to Chapters V and VI for complete procedures)
- How to avoid jar breakage
- What to do if you have a power failure
- Cooling jars
- Testing for seals
- What to do if lid didn't seal
- Storing canned food

Canning salt

Before food ripens in your garden, check on canning equipment (see Chapter III) and look over your canning directions and recipes so you can make a shopping list for canning. How much canning salt, sugar, spice and vinegar will you need?

Canning or pickling salt is recommended because it contains no additives. The iodine in most table salt reacts with starch in such foods as corn, often giving them a bluish color, and it may prevent normal fermentation of pickles and sauerkraut. The additive that prevents caking may make jars of vegetables appear cloudy .

Canning salt is usually available where canning supplies are sold. Do not store canning salt in a metal container; it reacts with metal and will corrode cans.

Although most people can vegetables with salt to add flavor and help retain texture and color, vegetables may be canned without salt. If you use a salt substitute, it is better to can vegetables without it, and use the salt substitute when you serve the vegetable.

Salt dissolves most readily if added to jars before adding vegetables. Salt sprinkled on top of a jar filled with whole tomatoes, for instance, may not dissolve completely, and when the jar is opened, the undissolved crystals may be mistaken for spoilage.

Methods of packing jars

There are two methods of packing food in canning jars.

Hot pack, the recommended method, means food is brought to a boil or cooked in an uncovered kettle for a specific length of time and then packed hot in jars.

Raw pack means raw, unheated food is packed in jars. This is an acceptable method for some foods—but not all.

Whether packed raw or hot, most food pieces are then covered with boiling water, syrup, juice or broth.

Hot packing usually results in a better product. One of the principles of canning is exhausting air from the jar—to get a vacuum seal. This means also removing air from food tissues, and heating food in an uncovered pan is the quickest way to drive out air. The rapid air removal from food tissue results in: fewer problems with light-colored foods turning dark near the top of the jar; less likelihood of fruits floating to the top of the jar; less likelihood of liquid boiling out during processing; fewer unsealed lids; better flavor retention.

Getting more food into fewer jars is another advantage of hot packing. When it's heated, food shrinks; this allows you to fill more into each jar without exceeding head space allowance. Research at The Pennsylvania State University in 1976 showed the weight of green beans in hot packed pint jars was 8.5 percent more than if jars were raw packed. A jar of hot packed apple slices showed a 25 percent increase in weight over apples packed raw.

Fruits and certain vegetables should be heated in a pot or blancher made of stainless steel or enamel to avoid noticeable darkening of food.

Overall work plan

You'll be happier on canning days if you don't have to cook a big meal, too. Plan simple but nutritious food for those days, and see how you can use the help of family members.

Clear countertops and work areas of all items not needed for canning. Think about where to place each item you'll be using—jars, lids, colander, cooling racks and other equipment. Set up an extra work surface if you need it.

Consider your time and energy. How much can you reasonably can each day? Wash and prepare only the amount of food that will fit in the canner at one time. Can early in the day when the kitchen is probably cooler and when you are fresh and alert.

Preparing jars and lids

Even if jars appear to be clean, they should be washed in hot sudsy water by hand or in a dishwasher. Rinse well—be particularly sure no detergent deposits remain on jars. (Alkaline detergents could cause color changes in some foods.) If you do not fill them immediately after washing, drain them upside down on a clean towel.

It is not necessary to sterilize empty jars which will be filled with food and sterilized in a pressure canner, or for 15 minutes or more in a boiling water canner. In these cases, jars will be sterilized along with the food. However, if food is to be sterilized less than 15 minutes in boiling water, the empty jars should be sterilized before filling.

To sterilize jars, place them right side up on a rack in a boiling water canner. Fill canner and jars with water to a level at least 1 inch above tops of jars. Boil 15 minutes; start counting time when water reaches an active rolling boil. If possible, remove one jar at a time, empty out the water, fill with food and adjust lid. If this is not possible, remove jars from boiling water after sterilizing and place them upside down on a clean towel to prevent microorganisms in the air from collecting in the jars.

Follow manufacturer's directions for preparing jar lids.

Selecting foods for canning

Since canning does not improve the quality of food, the first rule for success is to harvest or select sound, firm, ripe, fresh fruits and vegetables. Varieties most suitable for canning are listed in Chapters V and VI, where you'll also find specific directions for canning each one.

Fruits and tomatoes should be canned on the day they are best to eat fresh—in their prime. Vegetables should be young and tender, and canned the same day they're picked.

Discard *all* spoiled, diseased or bruised cherries, berries and plums—don't try to cut out blemishes. Remove any bruised or decayed parts on large fruits well below and around the defective areas—tissue may be soured. Any bit of spoiled food that gets canned may cause the entire jar of food to spoil later. At the very least, these unremoved bruised and decayed areas will show up as discolored spots, resulting in unattractive canned products of poor color, flavor and texture.

Washing fruits and vegetables

Dirt contains some of the bacteria hardest to kill, so a cardinal rule in canning is to wash thoroughly all food to be canned. Careful washing effectively reduces the load of spoilers; the fewer bacteria that ride into your canning jars on the food, the better. Sterilizing times are based on a reasonable population of bacteria to be destroyed. An enormous colony of spoilers might well survive recommended heat sterilizing times.

Before removing caps, stems, cores, pits, seeds or skins from fruits or vegetables, wash and agitate gently but thoroughly in several changes of water, or until water used in final rinse is clear. Lift food out of water each time so dirt that has been washed off doesn't get back on food. Do not let foods soak unnecessarily in water, and handle them gently to avoid bruising.

After peeling, coring, pitting or capping, rinse them gently again, or treat to prevent darkening (see below).

Treating to prevent darkening

There are several biochemical reactions of enzymes, oxygen and mild heat—singly or in combination—responsible for darkening fruits and vegetables. Most fresh fruits and vegetables contain both oxygen and enzymes. The enzymes are activated when the food is cut, bruised or crushed. Oxygen in the air causes oxidation and darkening; even the water used in canning contains a significant amount of dissolved oxygen. To prevent darkening and to preserve food, you have to destroy the enzymes and remove air from food tissues and from jars.

Heating food as quickly as possible after cutting destroys enzymes. But potatoes and fruits which darken quickly need prior treatment. Cut potatoes directly into a brine solution (1 teaspoon salt to 1 quart water). Submerge light-colored fruits such as apples, peaches and pears, in a solution of 2 tablespoons each vinegar and salt per gallon of water. Solutions of ascorbic acid or commercial antioxidant, such as Fruit-Fresh, may also be used. Follow directions on the label. Work fast: do not soak food more than 20 minutes. Drain and rinse before heating and/or packing in jars.

Heat to boiling the syrup or water used for packing foods in jars (directions follow). Boiling removes dissolved oxygen normally found in water and helps prevent darkening. Use the hot pack method—heating the food forces air and oxygen out of food tissues and juices.

Sugar and artificial sweeteners

Most fruits are canned with sugar. Sugar helps prevent spoilage in jams, jellies and preserves. It is not needed in other canned fruit except that it does help maintain color, texture and flavor. Sugar is usually added to jars as a syrup.

For special diets, fruits may be canned without sugar. But the use of artificial sweeteners in canning is not recommended because these products may change flavor and become bitter during sterilization and storage. Thus, it is better to can fruits without any sweetening, and add artificial sweetener when serving the fruit.

Sugar Syrup for Canned Fruit

Syrup	Recommended for	Sugar	Water	Yield
Light	small soft fruits	2 cups	4 cups	5 cups
Medium	peaches, apples, pears, sour berries	3 cups	4 cups	5½ cups
Heavy	all sour fruits	4¾ cups	4 cups	6½ cups

Allow 1 to 1½ cups syrup for each quart of fruit.

To make syrup, add sugar to water and bring to a boil while stirring. Reduce heat; keep syrup hot but do not boil as it will become too concentrated. Juice may be substituted for water if desired.

Use of heavy syrup is discouraged, unless you prefer extra sweet fruit. A medium syrup retains best color, shape, texture and flavor. But you'll save both money and calories if you can with a light syrup.

Preventing fruit from floating in jars

The volume of some fruits is nearly one third air and, if raw packed, they are most likely to float to the top of the jar. Heating fruit in syrup in an open kettle removes much of this air and fruit is less likely to float. Fruits are also less likely to float if packed in a light syrup. But even when hot pack and light syrup are used, some fruits may still float. However, after several weeks storage, the concentration of sugar in syrup and fruit will equalize and fruit may no longer float.

Filling jars

How tight to pack jars varies with individual foods; see specific directions in Chapters V and VI.

Hot food should be packed at or near boiling temperatures and covered with boiling liquid. Most raw food is also covered with boiling liquid. Covering food with liquid helps keep it from darkening.

Use a jar funnel to reduce spillage; try to keep liquid and grease off the sealing edge of the jar—this is especially important with liquids and meats. Use a serving spoon to pack peach, pear and apricot halves, cavity side down.

Allow head space as directed for specific foods.

The importance of head space

During heat sterilization, the food and liquid expands inside the jar. You allow for this expansion with a measured amount of air space—head space—between the lid and the top of the food or liquid in the jar.

Amount of head space varies with the product, style of pack and method of heat sterilization. Jellies, jams and preserves, packed hot, need only ⅛ inch (3 mm) head space. Pickles and relishes, juices, sauces and purees without meat, packed hot, need ¼ inch (6 to 7 mm) head space. Fruits and tomatoes, whether raw pack or hot pack, need ½ inch (12 to 13 mm) head space.

Because of greater expansion of foods which are sterilized in a pressure canner, head space specified for low-acid foods (vegetables and meats) will be greater—from 1 to 1¼ inches (25 to 32 mm).

Directions for canning each kind of food tell you how much head space to allow. It's important that you do this accurately. If you leave too little head space, expansion may force liquid out of jar, perhaps leaving food particles on the sealing edge and making a perfect seal impossible. Too much head space, on the other hand, leaves too much air inside the jar and increases discoloration of food.

After heat sterilization, you may observe increased head space in canned starchy vegetables; liquids are not lost but simply soaked up by these foods.

Releasing air bubbles

A better product results if all possible air is removed from inside canning jars. Sometimes air bubbles get trapped inside when you fill jars. To let them out, gently move a plastic spatula or knife up and down all around inside of jar. If you use a metal table knife to do this, don't let it hit the bottom of the jar. You may nick the glass and this weakens the jar, making it prone to breakage during heat sterilization. After releasing bubbles, readjust head space.

Closing jars

Use a clean, *damp* paper towel to remove food or liquid from the sealing edge of jars containing fruit. Use a clean, *dry* paper towel to remove residues from sealing edges of jars of vegetables and meats. Any food residue—especially fat—left on sealing surface could prevent lid from sealing.

To adjust lids, follow manufacturer's directions. Self-sealing lids are tightened before heat sterilization. Remember that 2-piece lids should have enough "give" to let air escape during heat sterilizing. Screw bands should be tight enough to hold jar lid closely to sealing edge, but not so tight as to prevent exhausting air. "Tighten firmly" expresses it best—but you know your own grip. If you notice large amounts of air bubbles inside jars, and/or discoloration of food near top of jars in storage, it's a signal that you may be tightening screw bands too much.

If lids are not self-sealing, directions call for final tightening after removing jars from canner.

Heat sterilizing

Regardless of lid manufacturer's instructions, use boiling water canner to sterilize all acid foods (fruits and tomatoes, pickles, relishes, jams, jellies and preserves). Use pressure canner to sterilize low-acid foods (vegetables and meats). *Do not do open kettle canning.*

Be suspicious of any new lids that direct you to use procedures for heat sterilizing in a boiling water bath at water levels below jar top. This results in inadequate sterilization and possible spoilage.

For complete directions, see Chapter V, Boiling Water Canning, and Chapter VI, Pressure Canning.

Jar breakage

Severe heat shock may cause jars to break. Never place raw pack jars abruptly in boiling water. Water in the canner should be hot, but not boiling. Bring it to a boil after adding jars. Hot pack jars may be placed in boiling water.

Jars in which peanut butter and other commercial products were packed should not be used. These jars are more susceptible to breakage than standard canning jars; they're not tempered sufficiently to withstand heat shock, nor are they strong enough to withstand quick pressure changes. Any jar with a small scratch or etch mark is prone to breakage and should not be used.

What to do if you have a power failure

There may be a brownout or a complete loss of power while you're heat sterilizing. If you use bottled gas, you may run out. Or someone may turn off or turn down your gas or electric unit without your realizing it. What do you do? For food safety, it is essential to complete the full heat sterilization schedule at the proper temperature.

If you have nearly completed the schedule when you lose energy, there may be enough residual heat to keep water boiling in a boiling water canner or to maintain a temperature of 240°F (115°C) in a pressure canner for the remainder of the sterilization time.

If energy is restored while jars are still warm but not sealed, discount any previous heating and heat sterilize the jars for the entire time specified, just as if they hadn't been sterilized at all.

If energy is not restored the same day, and if your refrigerator isn't affected, refrigerate jars overnight. (If it's an electric power failure, you may have to take jars to a friend's house.) The next day, replace lids with new ones, place jars in canner in cold water and reheat. When water reaches boiling (or pressure reaches desired level), heat sterilize jars for the full time specified for the product and jar size.

If you expect energy to be off longer than one day, try to arrange to sterilize jars in another home where power is available, or remove food from jars and freeze if possible.

If you notice, while heat sterilizing jars, that boiling stops or pressure drops because heat has been lowered for whatever reason, increase the heat until boiling or pressure returns. Discount any previous heating, reset timer and heat sterilize jars again the entire recommended time.

Obviously, food that must be reprocessed will be over-cooked, but better that than spoiled.

Cooling jars

Take jars from the canner and place them upright on a folded towel or rack, leaving at least 1 inch between jars so they will cool evenly on all sides. Do not touch lid. Avoid drafts. Retighten caps (or screw bands) *only* if recommended by lid manufacturer. Do not move jars for at least 12 hours, but preferably 24 hours.

Testing for seals

If you canned with recommended 2-piece metal lids, remove screw bands when jars are cool. If the lid is depressed or concave and will not move when pressed, and if it gives a clear ringing sound when tapped with a spoon, jars are sealed. If it sounds dull when tapped, it may indicate a poor seal—or just that food is touching jar lid. Check by turning jar on its side and rolling it. If there's no leakage, jar is airtight. Keep separate any jars that don't have a clear ringing sound; use them first if there are no signs of spoilage.

If you canned with rubber rings, turn jar on its side and roll it slowly to check for leakage.

What to do if lid didn't seal

If you find an unsealed jar within several hours after heat sterilization, there are three things you can do.

You can refrigerate the food and use it before spoilage takes place. You can freeze the food. Pack in freezer containers and label it to indicate that it was canned, then frozen, because it will not have as good color, texture and flavor as if frozen fresh.

The third alternative is to resterilize the food. Remove the lid and examine sealing surface of the jar. If not defective, adjust head space, clean sealing surface of jar, and put on a NEW lid and a different screw band. Heat sterilize again for the full time.

If the sealing surface of the jar is defective, empty food into another jar, use a new lid and sterilize again for the full time. Also, label the jar to indicate that food has been sterilized twice, because color, texture and flavor of such food will be less acceptable.

Storing canned food

Any food residue on the outside of the jar, especially on jar threads, will support growth of air-borne molds. During storage, some of these may penetrate the sealing compound and break the jar seal. To help prevent this, remove screw bands if using 2-piece metal lids, and wash jar body and jar threads gently. Wipe with a clean cloth. Label, date and store. If screw bands are left on jars, they may rust and be difficult to remove after storage.

Store canned food in a clean, cool, dark, dry area. Ideally, temperature should be above freezing, preferably between 40° and 50°F (5° and 10°C), but never above 95°F (35°C). You lose quality much faster when canned food is stored at high temperatures—70° to 95°F (21° to 35°C)—than at lower temperatures. Avoid storage in warm areas—near hot pipes, a hot water heater or furnace—and certainly keep jars out of direct sunlight.

Any light may cause darkening of canned food, especially fruits. Metal lids may rust in damp storage, which could result in pinholes in lids, breakage of seals and eventual spoilage of the food.

If canned foods are kept where there is danger of freezing, you could insulate jars by wrapping them in newspapers or blankets. Freezing does not cause spoilage, but if the seal is damaged or the jar broken, the food should not be eaten.

Periodically check jars in storage for signs of spoilage and other defects.

CHAPTER V

Canning Acid Foods in a Boiling Water Canner

Boiling water canning is recommended for heat sterilizing all fruits, tomatoes,* fermented and pickled vegetables, and jellies, jams and preserves sealed with lids. This table shows you how much fresh food you need to fill quart jars:

	Pounds per quart	Quarts per bushel
Apples	2½ to 3	16 to 20
Applesauce	2½ to 3½	15 to 18
Apricots	2 to 2½	20 to 24
Cherries	2 to 2½	22 to 32
Peaches	2 to 3	18 to 24
Pears	2 to 3	20 to 25
Plums	1½ to 2½	24 to 30
Tomatoes	2½ to 3½	15 to 20
Tomato juice	3 to 3½	12 to 16

*Tomatoes may be sterilized in pressure canner.

To produce high quality canned foods with good color, texture and flavor, choose a variety that cans well. If you have questions concerning a variety not mentioned or one that is localized, contact the Cooperative Extension Service in your county for up-to-date information on recommended canning varieties and maturity guidelines.

Sort fruits carefully and can only those of peak ripeness on any given day. The best stage of ripeness for canning is the same maturity you can enjoy for fresh eating. Normally a bushel of market-fresh fruit ripens over a three-day period and will require sorting and canning a portion daily.

ALTITUDE CORRECTIONS

Heat sterilization times given in the tables that follow are correct for altitudes of less than 1000 feet. If you are canning at higher altitudes, add the number of minutes specified for your altitude:

	If sterilization time is:	
Altitudes	**20 minutes or less**	**More than 20 minutes**
1000 feet	**add** 1 minute	**add** 2 minutes
2000 feet	2 minutes	4 minutes
3000 feet	3 minutes	6 minutes
4000 feet	4 minutes	8 minutes
5000 feet	5 minutes	10 minutes
6000 feet	6 minutes	12 minutes
7000 feet	7 minutes	14 minutes
8000 feet	8 minutes	16 minutes
9000 feet	9 minutes	18 minutes
10000 feet	10 minutes	20 minutes

For example: Directions for hot pack peaches call for 20 minutes for pints in boiling water canner, and 25 minutes for quarts. At 5000 feet, pints would be sterilized 20 minutes plus 5 minutes or 25 minutes. Quarts should be sterilized 25 minutes plus 10 minutes or 35 minutes.

Using the boiling water canner

Procedures and heat sterilization schedules for specific foods are given in alphabetical order in this section. Work only with the quantity of food needed for one canner load at one time. Prepare food and fill jars (see general directions in Chapter IV).

To use canner, put rack in bottom and fill canner half full with hot water. Cover and heat water to almost boiling.

Place jars of food on rack in canner. Add hot (not boiling) water to raise water level at least one inch, preferably two inches, above jar tops. Put cover on canner and quickly bring water to a rolling boil.

When water is boiling set timer for number of minutes required to heat sterilize the food being canned, and adjust heat to maintain a rolling boil throughout entire recommended time. Add more boiling water if needed to keep jars covered by at least one inch of boiling water.

Remove jars from canner as soon as heat sterilization is complete, and cool following directions in Chapter IV.

Apples

Hot pack, recommended method

• Select firm, sound apples, neither too green nor too ripe. Good varieties include Golden Delicious, Northern Spy, Winesap, Stayman, York Imperial, Rome Beauty, Jonathan, Yellow Newtown, Red Stele.

• Prepare jars and lids.

• Make syrup (recipe page 40).

• Wash, pare and core apples. Remove any bruised or decayed parts. To prevent darkening, slice directly into a solution of 2 tablespoons each salt and vinegar per gallon of water (or use solution of ascorbic acid or commercial antioxidant, following directions on package). Drain and rinse.

• Boil apples in syrup or water to cover 5 minutes.

• Pack hot in jar; cover with boiling syrup or water. Leave ½ inch head space.

• Remove air bubbles. Readjust head space.

• Wipe sealing edge of jar.

• Add and adjust lid.

- Sterilize in boiling water 20 minutes* for quarts; 15 minutes* for pints.
- Remove jars from canner. Cool. Test for seals and store (directions in Chapter IV).

Applesauce

Hot pack recommended method

- Select apples of proper maturity. If apples are too green, sauce will be gray color. If too ripe, sauce will be thin and runny. Sauce made from a blend of two varieties often has better texture and flavor. Good varieties include Early McIntosh, McIntosh, Golden Delicious, Northern Spy, Grimes Golden, Yellow Transparent, Winter Banana, York, Beacon, Tydemans Red, Yellow Newtown, Early Harvest, Lodi, Summer Rambo, Red Stele and Gravenstein.
- Prepare jars and lids.
- Wash, pare, quarter and core apples. Remove any bruised or decayed parts. To prevent darkening, drop into a solution of 2 tablespoons each salt and vinegar per gallon of water (or use solution of ascorbic acid or commercial antioxidant, following directions on package). Drain and rinse.
- Simmer, covered, in a small amount of water until tender.
- Press through sieve or food mill.
- Sweeten to taste, if desired.
- Reheat to boiling.
- Pack hot in jar. Leave ¼ inch head space.
- Remove air bubbles. Readjust head space.
- Wipe sealing edge of jar.
- Add and adjust lid.
- Sterilize in boiling water 15 minutes* for quarts or pints.
- Remove jars from canner. Cool. Test for seals and store (directions in Chapter IV).

Apricots

Hot pack, recommended method

- Select fruit with good flavor and color. Sort apricots. Each day can only those of maturity ideal for fresh eating. Handle

*See altitude corrections, page 47

gently to prevent bruising. Can with or without skins; whole, halved or sliced. Peeled, pitted apricots are best.
- Prepare jars and lids.
- Make syrup (recipe page 40).
- Wash apricots.
- To remove skins, heat in blancher basket submerged in boiling water. Heat *only* long enough to loosen skins, ½ to 1 minute (or slightly longer). Cool in cold water and drain. Apricots left too long in hot or cold water lose flavor, food value.
- Slip skins. Cut in half and remove pits. Remove any bruised or decayed parts. To prevent darkening, drop into a solution of 2 tablespoons each salt and vinegar per gallon of water (or use solution of ascorbic acid or commercial antioxidant, following directions on package). Drain and rinse.
- Heat to boiling in syrup or water to cover.
- Pack hot in jar. If canning halves, pack cavity side down; overlap halves. Cover with boiling syrup or water. Leave ½ inch head space.
- Remove air bubbles. Readjust head space.
- Wipe sealing edge of jar.
- Add and adjust lid.
- Sterilize in boiling water 25 minutes* for quarts; 20 minutes for pints.
- Remove jars from canner. Cool. Test for seals and store (directions in Chapter IV).

Raw pack, acceptable method
- Follow all preceding steps except do not heat apricots. Pack them raw in jars; cover with boiling syrup or water.
- Increase sterilizing time to 30 minutes* for quarts; 25 minutes* for pints.

Berries
Hot pack, recommended method for blackberries, blueberries and other firm berries.
- Select berries with good flavor and color; firm, but of proper maturity for eating fresh.

*See altitude corrections, page 47

- Prepare jars and lids.
- Sort and wash berries. Discard all spoiled, diseased or bruised berries. Remove stems, rinse and drain well.
- Place in kettle. Add ½ cup sugar for each quart fruit. Cover kettle and bring to boil; stir very gently to prevent crushing fruit and sticking.
- Pack hot in jar; cover with boiling syrup from cooking. Leave ½ inch head space.
- Remove air bubbles. Readjust head space.
- Wipe sealing edge of jar.
- Add and adjust lid.
- Sterilize in boiling water 15 minutes* for quarts or pints.
- Remove jars from canner. Cool. Test for seals and store (directions in Chapter IV).

Raw pack, recommended method for raspberries and other soft berries. Do not can strawberries; they have very poor texture.
- Make light syrup (page 40).
- Follow all preceding steps except do not heat berries; do not add sugar to berries. Pack raw in jars; shake down while filling. Cover with boiling syrup.
- Sterilize in boiling water 15 minutes* for quarts or pints.

Cherries
Hot pack, recommended method
- Select suitable variety of cherries, of uniform color and ideal maturity for eating fresh. Can cherries with or without pits, depending on how you plan to use them.
- Prepare jars and lids.
- Wash cherries. Discard all spoiled, bruised or diseased cherries and all that float—they may contain worms. Remove stems and rinse.
- Remove pits from sour cherries; also from sweet cherries if desired.

*See altitude corrections, page 47

- Place in kettle. Add ½ cup sugar for each quart fruit. Add a little water to unpitted cherries to keep them from sticking while heating. Cover kettle and bring to a boil.
- Pack hot in jar; cover with boiling syrup from cooking. Leave ½-inch head space.
- Remove air bubbles. Readjust head space.
- Wipe sealing edge of jar.
- Add and adjust lid.
- Sterilize in boiling water 15 minutes* for quarts or pints.
- Remove jars from canner. Cool. Test for seals and store (directions in Chapter IV).

Raw pack, acceptable method
- Make light syrup (page 40).
- Follow all preceding steps except do not heat cherries; do not add sugar to cherries. Pack raw in jars; shake down while filling. Cover with boiling syrup.
- Increase sterilizing time to 25 minutes* for quarts; 20 minutes* for pints.

Fruit Butters
Hot pack, recommended method
- Select sound ripe fruit—apples, apricots, peaches, pears or plums.
- Prepare jars and lids. Can in pint and half-pint jars only.
- Sterilize jars.
- Wash fruit. Remove skins and any bruised or decayed parts. Remove pits and cut fruit in pieces.
- Simmer until soft in just enough cider, juice or water to prevent sticking.
- Put fruit through sieve or food mill.
- Cook pulp until thick enough to hold its shape on spoon; stir to prevent sticking.
- Add 2 cups sugar to each quart pulp. Add ground cinnamon and ground cloves to taste.
- Simmer until thick enough to spread; stir to prevent sticking.
- Pack hot in sterilized jar. Leave ¼ inch head space.

*See altitude corrections, page 47

- Remove air bubbles. Readjust head space.
- Wipe sealing edge of jar.
- Add and adjust lid.
- Sterilize in boiling water 10 minutes* for pints or half-pints.
- Remove jars from canner. Cool. Test for seals and store (directions in Chapter IV).

Fruit Juices

Hot pack, recommended method
- Select quality fruits that are ripe and juicy, flavorful and free of disease.
- Prepare jars and lids.
- Wash fruit. Remove skins and any bruised or decayed parts. Remove pits and crush.
- Heat to simmering. Strain through cloth bag.
- Add sugar if desired—about 1 cup per gallon of juice, depending on sweetness of juice.
- Reheat to simmering.
- Fill jar. Leave ¼ inch head space.
- Wipe sealing edge of jar.
- Add and adjust lid.
- Sterilize in boiling water 15 minutes* for quarts or pints.
- Remove jars from canner. Cool. Test for seals and store (directions in Chapter IV).

Fruit Purees

Hot pack, recommended method
- Select sound ripe fruit.
- Prepare jars and lids.
- Wash fruits. Remove skins and any bruised or decayed parts. Remove pits. Cut large fruits in pieces.

*See altitude corrections, page 47

- Simmer until soft. Add small amount of water if needed, to prevent sticking.
- Put fruit through sieve or food mill.
- Add sugar to taste.
- Simmer to desired consistency.
- Pack hot in jar. Leave ¼ inch head space.
- Remove air bubbles. Readjust head space.
- Wipe sealing edge of jar.
- Add and adjust lid.
- Sterilize in boiling water 15 minutes* for quarts or pints.
- Remove jars from canner. Cool. Test for seals and store (directions in Chapter IV).

Jams, Jellies, Preserves
Hot pack, recommended when using 2-piece lids
- Prepare jars and lids.
- Sterilize jars.
- Choose recipe using commercial pectin. Carefully wash fruit. Remove any bruised or decayed part. Regardless of recipe directions, remove skins or peels from peaches, apricots, pears and apples as these may contribute to spoilage by molds.
- Follow recipe to make jam, jelly or preserves.
- Pack hot in *sterilized* jar. Leave ⅛ inch head space.
- Wipe sealing edge of jar.
- Add and adjust lid.
- Sterilize in boiling water for 5 minutes.*
- Remove jars from canner. Cool. Test for seals and store (directions in Chapter IV).

Peaches
Hot pack, recommended method
- Select freestone variety with skin that slips off easily after scalding. Sweetness, flavor and texture are important criteria. Good yellow varieties include Triogem, Redhaven,

---

*See altitude corrections, page 47

Redskin, Sunhigh and Rio Oso Gem. Elbertas are slightly less desirable. Good white varieties include Early Red Free, Raritan Rose, White Giant, Laterose, Champion, Summerrose, White Hale and Belle of Georgia. Preferred varieties may be available for only a week or so. Each day can only those of maturity ideal for fresh eating. Handle carefully to prevent bruising.

- Prepare jars and lids.
- Make syrup (recipe page 40).
- Wash peaches.
- To remove skins, heat in blancher basket submerged in boiling water. Heat only long enough to loosen skins, ½ to 1 minute (or slightly longer). Cool in cold water and drain. Peaches left too long in hot or cold water lose flavor and food value.
- Slip skins. Cut in half and remove pits. Also remove any bruised or decayed parts. Slice if desired. To prevent darkening, drop into a solution of 2 tablespoons each salt and vinegar per gallon of water (or use solution of ascorbic acid or commercial antioxidant, following directions on package). Drain and rinse.
- Heat to boiling in syrup or water to cover.
- Pack hot in jar. If canning halves, pack cavity side down; overlap halves. Cover with boiling syrup or water. Leave ½ inch head space.
- Remove air bubbles. Readjust head space.
- Wipe sealing edge of jar.
- Add and adjust lid.
- Sterilize in boiling water 25 minutes* for quarts; 20 minutes* for pints.
- Remove jars from canner. Cool. Test for seals and store (directions in Chapter IV).

Raw pack, acceptable method
- Follow all preceding steps except do not heat peaches. Pack them raw in jars; cover with boiling syrup or water.
- Increase sterilizing time to 30 minutes* for quarts; 25 minutes* for pints.

---

*See altitude corrections, page 47

Pears

Hot pack, recommended method

● Select suitable variety for canning. Bartlett pears remain the home canner's choice. Keiffer pears make good canned products, but must be fully ripe before canning. Other recommended varieties include Flemish Beauty, Gorham, Winter Neles, Seckel and Wordenseckel. Fruit ready for eating is ready for canning. Each day, sort and can only those of proper maturity.

● Prepare jars and lids.

● Make syrup (recipe page 40).

● Wash and pare; cut pears in half and core. Use a melon ball cutter or measuring teaspoon to remove cores. Remove any bruised or decayed parts. Slice if desired. To prevent darkening, slice directly into a solution of 2 tablespoons each salt and vinegar per gallon of water (or use solution of ascorbic acid or commercial antioxidant, following directions on package). Drain and rinse.

● Heat to boiling in syrup or water to cover.

● Pack hot in jar. If canning halves, pack cavity side down; overlap halves. Cover with boiling syrup or water. Leave ½ inch head space.

● Wipe sealing edge of jar.

● Add and adjust lid.

● Sterilize in boiling water 25 minutes* for quarts; 20 minutes* for pints.

● Remove jars from canner. Cool. Test for seals and store (directions in Chapter IV).

Raw pack, acceptable method

● Follow all preceding steps except do not heat pears. Pack them raw in jars; cover with boiling syrup or water.

● Increase sterilizing time to 30 minutes* for quarts; 25 minutes* for pints.

---

*See altitude corrections, page 47

Pineapple
Hot pack, recommended method
- Select ripe, but not overripe pineapple.
- Prepare jars and lids.
- Make syrup (recipe page 40).
- Peel pineapple and cut as for serving.
- Simmer in syrup, juice or water until tender.
- Pack hot in jar. Cover with boiling liquid. Leave ½ inch head space.
- Remove air bubbles. Readjust head space.
- Wipe sealing edge of jar.
- Add and adjust lid.
- Sterilize in boiling water 20 minutes* for quarts; 15 minutes* for pints.
- Remove jars from canner. Cool. Test for seals and store (directions in Chapter IV).

Raw pack, acceptable method
- Follow all preceding steps except do not heat pineapple. Pack pieces raw in jars; cover with boiling syrup, juice or water.
- Increase sterilizing time to 30 minutes* for quarts or pints.

Plums
Hot pack, recommended method
- Select variety with good flavor and color—Gages or Damsons or one of the following prune plums: Stanley, Bluefree, President, Imperial Epineuse, Fellenberg, German and Hungarian. Fruit ready for eating is ready for canning. Each day, sort and can only those of proper maturity.
- Prepare jars and lids.
- Make syrup (recipe page 40.)
- Wash plums. Discard all spoiled, diseased or bruised fruit.

*See altitude corrections, page 47

- Can whole or halved. If freestone, remove pits. If canned whole, prick skins with fork to prevent fruit from bursting when heated.
- Heat to boiling in syrup or juice to cover.
- Pack hot in jar. Cover with boiling syrup or juice. Leave ½ inch head space.
- Remove air bubbles. Readjust head space.
- Wipe sealing edge of jar.
- Add and adjust lid.
- Sterilize in boiling water 25 minutes* for quarts; 20 minutes* for pints.
- Remove jars from canner. Cool. Test for seals and store (directions in Chapter IV).

Raw pack, acceptable method
- Follow all preceding steps except do not heat plums. Pack raw in jar. Cover with boiling syrup or juice.
- Sterilize in boiling water 25 minutes* for quarts; 20 minutes* for pints.

Rhubarb
Hot pack, recommended method
- Can rhubarb in early spring or late fall when level of oxalic acid is low. Select tender, young stalks. Remove leaves. Can immediately after picking.
- Prepare jars and lids.
- Wash and trim. Cut stems in ½-inch pieces.
- Add ½ cup sugar for each quart rhubarb. Let stand to draw out juice.
- Heat to boiling.
- Pack hot in jar. Leave ½ inch head space.
- Remove air bubbles. Readjust head space.
- Wipe sealing edge of jar.
- Add and adjust lid.
- Sterilize in boiling water 15 minutes* for quarts or pints.

*See altitude corrections, page 47

• Remove jars from canner. Cool. Test for seals and store (directions in Chapter IV).

The truth about low-acid tomatoes

Acidity of new tomato varieties and their relationship to a possible outbreak of botulism have been in the news. After considerable investigation, it appears that most home canned tomatoes spoil—not because they're "low-acid"—but because heat sterilization was too short, or open kettle canning or other unacceptable canning procedures were used.

New varieties of tomatoes which taste less acid are being grown. However, taste can be deceiving, especially with pear-shaped and yellow tomatoes. You cannot determine the acidity of a tomato by its taste. That's because there are different kinds of acids; apples, for example, are true acid foods, but do not taste as acid as citrus fruit. Recent research shows that, even though some new tomatoes are referred to as low-acid, pH values are no different than traditional varieties.

Most directions for canning tomatoes in print as late as 1975—and some 1976 directions, too—give heat sterilization schedules which are too short for tomato products using any kind of tomato. (Refer to the discussion of botulism in Chapter II, especially the footnote.) Sterilizing schedules that follow are adequate for all tomatoes, and there is no need to add lemon juice or vinegar. However, you will doubtless see news stories suggesting this, and if you wish to acidify your tomatoes, you may add 1 teaspoon bottled concentrated lemon juice or standard vinegar (5 percent acid strength) to each pint of whole or quartered tomatoes, tomato juice or puree (2 teaspoons per quart). Or use citric acid U.S.P., ¼ teaspoon for pints, ½ teaspoon for quarts. As another option, tomatoes may be packed hot in jars and sterilized in a pressure canner for 10 minutes at 5 pounds pressure for both quarts and pints.*

*Correct for high altitude as follows: 2000 feet, 5.5 pounds; 4000 feet, 6 pounds; 6000 feet, 6.5 pounds; 8000 feet, 7 pounds; 10000 feet, 7.5 pounds.

Tomatoes (whole or quartered)

Hot pack, recommended method

- Select tomatoes of proper maturity—neither overly ripe nor green. They should be picked when uniformly red but still firm. When necessary they may be held several days, out of the sun, before canning. Better varieties are crack-resistant, uniform, medium size and have excellent color and flavor. They include Campbell 1327, Heinz 1350, 1370 and 1439, New Yorker, Spring Giant, Ace 55VF, Vineripe VFN and Ramapo.
- Prepare jars and lids.
- Wash tomatoes; handle gently to avoid bruising. Those with large decayed areas or diseased cracks are unfit for canning. Trim away small decayed spots.
- To remove skins, heat in blancher basket submerged in boiling water. Heat only long enough to loosen skins, about ½ minute (or slightly longer). Cool in cold water and drain. Tomatoes left in hot or cold water lose flavor and food value.
- Remove skins and cores, making sure all the white part of the core is removed. Trim out green spots.
- Place in kettle and heat to boiling. Do not add water. Stir to prevent sticking.
- Pack hot in jar, adding 1 teaspoon salt per quart if desired. Cover with boiling juice. Leave ½ inch head space.
- Remove air bubbles. Readjust head space.
- Wipe sealing edge of jar.
- Add and adjust lid.
- Sterilize in boiling water 45 minutes* for quarts; 35 minutes* for pints.
- Remove jars from canner. Cool. Test for seals and store (directions in Chapter IV).

Raw pack, acceptable method

- Follow all preceding steps except do not heat tomatoes. Pack raw in jar; press gently to fill spaces, or add boiling tomato juice. Do not add water.
- Increase sterilizing time to 50 minutes* for quarts; 40 minutes* for pints.

---

*See altitude corrections, page 47

Separation of canned tomato products

This is a common problem—especially in tomato juice—and it can't always be prevented. What you see is a watery, pale-color layer of liquid, free of solids, near the top and/or the bottom of the jar. In no way does separation indicate spoilage, but for aesthetic reasons, such juice should be shaken vigorously just before serving.

What causes it? Fresh tomatoes contain both enzymes and pectins. When tomatoes are cut, crushed or bruised, and exposed to air, the enzymes are activated. One of the things they do is break down the pectins and this causes juice to separate. (Before they're broken down, pectins are similar to the chemical substances that give texture to jams, jellies and preserves.)

Enzymes are easily destroyed by heat. So if you heat tomatoes quickly, as soon as you cut them and before you extract juice, you can minimize the enzyme action on the pectins . . . and thus minimize juice separation.

Use this method: Wash and sort enough tomatoes for one canner load of jars. Cut out diseased areas but do not peel or core. Begin by quartering enough of the tomatoes to make about 1 quart of juice (about 3 pounds tomatoes). Place quartered tomatoes in an 8-quart (or larger) kettle without water, and heat rapidly to boiling while stirring and crushing them. Keep high heat under kettle. Work rapidly and continue to add quartered tomatoes at a rate slow enough to sustain boiling temperatures. Stir and crush tomatoes at frequent intervals. Five minutes after all tomatoes have been added to kettle, remove from heat, press juice, reheat *just to boiling* and fill hot in jars according to directions that follow.

Note that juice separation, especially at the top of the jars, is even more pronounced if juice is boiled too long before filling hot into jars.

Starting with firm, ripe tomatoes also minimizes separation. Avoid watery, overmature or soft fruit. And DO use the hot pack method.

Tomato Juice
Hot pack, recommended method
- Select red-ripe juicy tomatoes. Good varieties include all those listed for whole tomatoes plus Better Boy VFN and Supersonic.
- Prepare jars and lids.
- Wash tomatoes. Trim away any small bruised or decayed spots. Tomatoes with large decayed areas or diseased cracks are unfit for juice.
- Remove stem ends and cut in quarters. Work fast; juice is less likely to separate if tomatoes are heated as soon as possible after cutting (see preceding paragraphs).
- Simmer until softened, stirring often.
- Put through sieve or food mill. Add 1 teaspoon salt per quart if desired.
- Reheat at once until just boiling.
- Fill jar with boiling hot juice. Leave ¼ inch head space.
- Wipe sealing edge of jar.
- Add and adjust lid.
- Sterilize in boiling water 35 minutes* for quarts and pints.
- Remove jars from canner. Cool. Test for seals, and store (directions in Chapter IV).

Tomato Sauce or Puree
(No other vegetable and no meat added)
Hot pack, recommended method
- Select pear type tomatoes such as Roma VF, San Marzano, Red Top, Chico III, Royal Chico; or use varieties recommended for whole tomatoes.
- Prepare jars and lids. Can in pint or half-pint jars only.
- Wash tomatoes. Those with large decayed areas or diseased cracks are unfit for canning. Trim away any small bruised or decayed parts.
- Remove stem ends, quarter and simmer until softened, following directions for tomato juice.
- Put through sieve or food mill.

*See altitude corrections, page 47

- Simmer until sauce thickens to desired consistency, stirring frequently.
- Fill hot in pint jars only, adding ½ teaspoon salt per pint if desired. Leave ¼ inch head space.
- Remove air bubbles. Readjust head space.
- Wipe sealing edge of jar.
- Add and adjust lid.
- Sterilize in boiling water. Sterilization schedule depends on consistency or thickness of sauce. Sterilize thin sauce 35 minutes* for pints or half-pints. Sterilize thick sauce (simmered to half original volume) 20 minutes* for pints or half-pints.
- Remove jars from canner. Cool. Test for seals, and store (directions in Chapter IV).

Tomato Sauce or Puree
(With other vegetables added but no meat added)
Hot pack, recommended method
- Follow all preceding steps except make tomato sauce or puree by cooking other vegetables (such as peppers or onions) with tomatoes. Press through a sieve or food mill and simmer until pulp is thick (reduced to half the volume).
- Increase sterilizing time to 45 minutes* for pints or half-pints.

For Tomato Sauce with Meat, see Chapter VI.

---

*See altitude corrections, page 47

PICKLES AND RELISHES

It used to be that good home canned pickles and kraut were a product of real skill and luck. Old recipes were considered good even if they failed once in a while. If Grandma had success with her recipes, it was because they were matched to the kind of vinegar she made—strong or weak— and because she gave daily attention to her art: controlling the salt concentration and temperature, and removing surface scum during fermentation.

Today, any careful home canner should be able to make top quality pickles and sauerkraut. But for many, fermented and pickled vegetables still cause more problems than any other home canned food. There are several reasons for this. Old recipe formulations and use of homemade vinegar are sometimes at fault. Failure may be caused by use of unsuitable varieties or maturities of cucumbers and cabbage and the use of iodized salt. Spoilage may result from failure to provide proper fermenting temperatures or to remove surface scum daily during pickling.

Perhaps at fault most often is the use of recipes which give directions for open kettle canning or too little heat treatment for sterilizing these products.

Still another reason for failure is borderline acidity which may be caused by use of hard water (which is alkaline) or by the addition of lime to firm the pickled product. Some old recipes don't have enough acidity to offset the effects of lime or very hard water on pH.

Properly fermented and pickled vegetables are acid foods, have a pH normally between 3.6 and 4.2, and when canned are sterilized easily in a boiling water canner. However, if errors (such as those described above) result in a product with a pH of 4.6 or higher, such product would have to be considered a low-acid food and would require sterilization treatments in a pressure canner similar to fresh vegetables.

For successfully fermented and pickled foods, use a modern recipe. You can identify a modern recipe (or a modern recipe book) by these criteria:
• Recipe specifies the use of standard vinegar of 5 percent acidity (50 grains).

- Recipe uses hot pack method, especially filling with boiling hot brine, liquor or pickling syrup.
- Recipe specifically directs you to heat sterilize or process the filled jars in a boiling water canner; it does not endorse open kettle canning.
- Recipe directs you to sterilize pickles and relishes for 15 minutes (or more) in a boiling water bath—or to use sterilized jars if sterilizing less than 15 minutes.

(Some pickles would be overcooked or of poor quality if sterilized too long. However, it is important that jars get a full 15 minutes in a boiling water bath—thus the direction to use sterilized jars if recommended sterilizing time for the pickles is less than 15 minutes.)

Good recipes include those in *Farm Journal's Homemade Pickles and Relishes** and in canning publications available from major lid and jar manufacturers. Any favorite family recipe which has given *consistently good results* without incidence of spoilage is also evidence of an acceptable recipe.

Use pure salt—pickling or canning salt—to make pickles. Iodized salt may darken pickles and retard natural fermentation. Table salt contains additives to prevent caking and these may make brine cloudy.

If you suspect that hard water may be the cause of your trouble, look for a new recipe—one with a higher proportion of vinegar and sugar. Your County Extension Home Economist may have recipes better suited to water in your area.

When you brine pickles, use only suitable containers such as domestic stoneware crocks (some foreign-made crocks have glazes high in lead), glass, stainless steel, unchipped enamelware, or food-grade plastic such as polyethelene. DO NOT USE wooden or other metal containers or any container that is chipped or cracked.

Cucumbers used for pickles should be a pickling variety; this will be noted on seed packet or in seed catalog. Slicing cucumbers and waxed cucumbers are not suitable for pickles. Cucumbers should be picked when slightly immature and of desired size and used the same day they're picked. After scrubbing and rinsing cucumbers, trim ⅛-inch slice from

---

*Published in 1976 by Countryside Press, a division of Farm Journal, Inc., Philadelphia, Pa.

both ends. This cuts away enzymes that may otherwise cause soft pickles.

Based on ingredients used and the method of preparation, there are five kinds of pickle products, described below. They are: *fermented pickles, cured pickles, quick process pickles, fruit pickles* and *relishes.*

Fermented Pickles (in brine)

Before they are canned, fermented pickles go through a curing and fermenting process which takes about 3 to 5 weeks, depending on room temperature. The vegetables (usually cucumbers) are submerged in brine. While the salt in the brine prevents spoilage, natural bacterial action changes the sugar in cucumbers to acids. Lactic acid is the major acid formed during fermentation and it is responsible for much of the desirable flavor.

Strength of the brine is extremely imporant. Your recipe will doubtless give directions for maintaining a 10 percent brine solution. If brine is too strong in the beginning, it inhibits growth of bacteria that produce lactic acid; the result is poorly flavored, shriveled pickles. If the brine is too weak, the desirable bacteria are overcome by spoilage bacteria and pickles become slippery and don't taste good. Maintaining the proper brine strength is a key step in fermenting cucumbers. Salt draws moisture from the cucumbers and this dilutes the brine—it becomes weaker. Therefore, a good recipe will tell you the proper amount of salt to use initially, and how much more salt to add during the fermentation period.

Vegetables tend to float in the brine, so they must be forcibly submerged all during the fermentation process. Hold them down with a heavy plate or glass lid—one that's big enough to cover the cucumbers, but small enough to fit inside the crock. Lay a weight on the plate—a glass jug filled with water makes a good weight.

The right room temperature also encourages the activity of desirable bacteria . . . between 65° and 75°F (18° and 24°C) is ideal.

During fermentation, scum forms on top of the brine. This scum is made up of yeasts, molds and bacteria in the air. It must be removed daily so that it won't interfere with the fermentation process.

Even though the fermentation process usually gives cucumbers the desired acidity (or pH level), some recipes call for the addition of vinegar. For good results, use a modern recipe and follow all steps carefully.

Sauerkraut is fermented cabbage. To make good sauerkraut, follow directions in a modern recipe very carefully.

Cured Pickles

Recipes for *cured pickles* begin with directions for soaking cucumbers in a brine which may or may not have vinegar added, for 1 to 5 days. After this, they may be soaked again in a vinegar solution with spices or other seasonings. Use a recipe which specifies standard vinegar with 5 percent acidity. Don't reduce the amount of vinegar in the recipe or in any way change the proportion of vinegar to vegetable. Follow directions carefully.

Quick Process Pickles

Vinegar gives *quick process pickles* the necessary acidity which fermentation provides in the pickles described earlier. Their flavor comes from the acetic acid in vinegar, rather than lactic acid formed by fermentation. Use standard vinegar with 5 percent acidity, not homemade vinegar. Don't reduce the amount of vinegar given or change the proportion of vinegar to vegetable in your recipe. Follow directions exactly for best results.

Fruit Pickles and Relishes

Vinegar also provides the required acidity for good fruit pickles and relishes; sugar and spices add the characteristic flavors. Use whole fruit or pieces for fruit pickles; chopped vegetables or fruits for relishes. Recipes will direct you to simmer them in the sweetened vinegar syrup. Use modern recipes; follow them exactly; do not change the strength (acidity) of the syrup, nor the proportion of vinegar to solids.

CHAPTER VI

Canning Low-Acid Foods in a Pressure Canner

Pressure canning is essential for heat sterilizing all fresh vegetables (except tomatoes), and all meat, poultry, fish, stews, soup and meat sauces.* This table tells you how much fresh food you need to fill quart jars:

	Pounds per quart	Quarts per bushel
Asparagus	2½ to 4¼	10 to 12
Beans, lima, in pods	3 to 5	6 to 10
Beans, green or wax	1½ to 2½	12 to 20
Beets, without tops	2 to 3⅓	15 to 24
Carrots, without tops	2 to 3	16 to 25
Corn, sweet, in husks	3 to 6	6 to 10
Peas, green, in pods	3 to 6	5 to 10
Pumpkin or winter squash	1½ to 3	----
Spinach & other greens	2 to 6	3 to 8
Squash, summer	2 to 4	10 to 20

*The proper heat sterilization schedule for stews, soups, and meat sauces is the time for the food requiring longest heat sterilization time. Tomatoes may be sterilized in a pressure canner.

To produce high quality canned foods with good color, texture and flavor, choose a variety that cans well. If you have questions concerning a variety not mentioned or one that is localized, contact the Cooperative Extension Service in your county for up-to-date information on recommended canning varieties and maturity guidelines.

Vegetables should be of proper maturity and top quality. They should be canned as soon as possible after picking.

Procedures and heat sterilization schedules for specific foods are given in this section . . . vegetables first in alphabetical order, then meats and meat sauces. Work only with the quantity of food needed for one canner load at one time. Prepare food and fill jars (directions in Chapter IV).

Using a pressure canner

Before you use a pressure canner, study directions carefully in the use-and-care booklet packed with your canner. Make sure you understand each part and how to use it. Review information about pressure canners in Chapter III.

Put rack in canner and add 2 or 3 inches of hot water. Set filled jars on rack. Fasten cover securely. Place canner over heat.

With a dial gauge canner: To remove air from canner (this is called "exhausting"), leave vent open and bring water to a boil. As water boils, steam forces air from vent. When steam starts escaping steadily, allow about 10 minutes to exhaust all air.

It is essential that all air be removed to get an accurate indication of pressure on the dial gauge, which, in turn, tells you that you have achieved the sterilization temperature you need. At sea level, 10 pounds pressure translates to 240°F (115°C).

When steam is nearly invisible 1 to 2 inches above vent, it means air has been removed. Close the vent and continue heating until pressure climbs to 10 pounds (more for altitudes 2000 feet or higher—see Altitude Chart that follows).

When required pressure is reached, start counting sterilization time. Do not leave canner untended. Regulate heat to maintain pressure at or slightly above needed pressure for entire heat sterilization time for the food, style of pack, packing method and size of jar. If pressure is too low it means temperature is too low, and heat sterilization may not be adequate to destroy heat resistant bacteria that may be present on food.

If you allow pressure to fluctuate significantly, liquid may be forced from jars.

With a weighted gauge canner: To remove air from canner, leave vent open and bring water to a boil. As water boils, steam forces air from vent. When steam starts escaping steadily, allow about 10 minutes to exhaust all air.

Close vent with weighted gauge, being sure you set it in correct position to regulate pressure at 10 pounds. Continue heating; the gauge will jiggle when it reaches selected pressure. Start counting sterilization time when it jiggles at least 2 or 3 times a minute. A jiggle means several quick sounds in a 5-second interval, releasing steam. There should be 2 of these per minute. No altitude adjustment is needed with weighted gauge canners. Regulate heat so weight jiggles 2 or 3 times per minute during entire sterilization period. If it jiggles more often, it means you're using more heat than is necessary.

Cooling canner

When sterilization time is completed, remove canner from heat to cool—this will take at least 30 minutes and possibly a full hour for large canners.

Do not open air vent until canner has cooled and pressure is zero. If you open it prematurely, the sudden change in pressure may force liquid from the jars.

Do not put canner in or under cold water to speed cooling. This, too, would cause loss of liquid from jars. The sudden cooling might also warp lid and damage it permanently.

After proper cooling period, remove weight or open vent. Then wait 2 minutes before unlocking lid. Remove it carefully, tilting the far side up first in a position to shield your face from escaping steam.

Remove jars from canner and cool, following directions in Chapter IV.

Keep a time-log

To help you plan your time in the kitchen, figure in an extra hour beyond the recommended heat sterilization time for the food you are canning. This covers 10 minutes for exhausting, 5 minutes to build up pressure and from 30 to 60 minutes to cool the canner before you can open it again.

Write down the exact time when canner reaches desired pressure, and add the number of minutes recommended for the food and size jar you are sterilizing. This gives you the time to take canner off heat. For example, if you achieve pressure at 9:35 and you are to sterilize food for 1 hour 15 minutes, you'll finish at 10:50. You might want to set your timer for the last 15 minutes—just to be sure.

Experienced canners also keep notes on heat settings needed to maintain pressure, so they can turn range burner to the right setting as soon as they have achieved pressure.

ALTITUDE CORRECTIONS

If you have a dial gauge canner and are canning at altitudes 2000 feet or above, you must heat the canner sufficiently to sustain higher pressure as shown on the chart below. (Weighted gauge canners adjust automatically for altitude variations.)

At altitudes of:	Maintain pressure at:
2000 feet	11 pounds
4000 feet	12 pounds
6000 feet	13 pounds
8000 feet	14 pounds
10000 feet	15 pounds

For example: Directions call for 10 pounds pressure. At 6000 feet, dial gauge must indicate 13 pounds to equal same temperature at sea level. Time remains the same.

Asparagus

Hot pack, recommended method

- Asparagus should be tender and freshly picked.
- Prepare jars and lids.
- Wash. Break off tough ends and trim off scales. Wash several times to remove all sand or other soil.
- Cut in 1-inch pieces, or can as whole spears.
- Heat in blancher basket submerged in boiling water; boil 2 or 3 minutes.
- Pack hot in jar, adding 1 teaspoon salt per quart if desired. Cover with boiling water. Leave 1 inch head space.
- Remove air bubbles. Readjust head space.
- Wipe sealing edge of jar.
- Add and adjust lid.
- Sterilize at 10 pounds pressure* 30 minutes for quarts; 25 minutes for pints.
- Cool canner before opening vent.
- Wait 2 minutes; remove lid.
- Remove jars from canner. Cool. Test for seals and store (directions in Chapter IV).

Raw pack, acceptable method

- Follow all preceding steps except do not blanch. Pack raw in jar, as tight as possible without crushing. Cover with boiling water.
- Sterilize as for hot pack.

Beans, Lima

Hot pack, recommended method

- Select suitable variety for canning, such as Baby Fordhook, Fordhook 242, Early Thorogreen, Thaxter, Bridgeton. Can only tender beans, freshly picked.
- Prepare jars and lids.
- Wash, shell and rinse again.
- Put in blancher basket, submerge in boiling water, and boil 3 minutes.

*For dial gauge, see altitude corrections, page 72.

- Pack hot, loosely in jar, adding 1 teaspoon salt per quart if desired. Cover with boiling water. Leave 1 inch head space.
- Remove air bubbles. Readjust head space.
- Wipe sealing edge of jar.
- Add and adjust lid.
- Sterilize at 10 pounds pressure* 50 minutes for quarts; 40 minutes for pints.
- Cool canner before opening vent.
- Wait 2 minutes; remove lid.
- Remove jars from canner. Cool. Test for seals and store (directions in Chapter IV).

Raw pack, acceptable method
- Follow all preceding steps except do not blanch. Pack raw, very loosely in jar; do not press or shake down. Cover with boiling water.
- Sterilize as for hot pack.

Beans, Snap, Green or Wax
Hot pack, recommended method
- Select suitable variety for canning. Bush Blue Lake, a white seeded variety, has excellent color, flavor and texture. Tenderette (white seeded) and Tendercrop (dark seeded) are also good choices. Other recommended varieties include Blue Lake Stringless and Romano pole beans; Early Gallatin bush beans; and any of the following wax beans: Kinghorn Wax, Goldcrop, SinClair, Butterwax, Midas and Bonanza. Pick when they are tender and snap readily. Can the same day. Over-mature beans may be tough and stringy.
- Prepare jars and lids.
- If quite dirty, wash before snapping. Otherwise, snap before washing. Wash until last rinse is clear; lift beans from water after each washing. Snap or break ends off. Cut or snap into pieces about 1½ inches if desired. Heat in blancher basket submerged in boiling water and boil 3 minutes.
- Pack hot, loosely in jar, adding 1 teaspoon salt per quart if desired. Cover with boiling water. Leave 1 inch head space.
- Remove air bubbles. Readjust head space.
- Wipe sealing edge of jar.
- Add and adjust lid.

---

*For dial gauge, see altitude corrections, page 72.

- Sterilize at 10 pounds pressure* 25 minutes for quarts; 20 minutes for pints.
- Cool canner before opening vent.
- Wait 2 minutes; remove lid.
- Remove jars from canner. Cool. Test for seals and store (directions in Chapter IV).

Raw pack, acceptable method
- Follow all preceding steps except do not blanch. Pack raw, tightly in jar. Cover with boiling water.
- Sterilize as for hot pack.

Beets
Hot pack, recommended method
- Select suitable variety for canning including Ruby Queen, strains of Detroit Dark Red, Firechief, Honey Red, Red Pack. For best quality, harvest or buy *fresh* beets from 1 to 1½ inches in diameter. Can same day.
- Prepare jars and lids.
- Sort for size, and can same size together. Cut off leaves, leaving 1 inch of stem and root to prevent excessive color loss. Wash off dirt with garden hose if possible and scrub well with good brush. Rinse in several changes of water until rinse water is clear.
- Cover with boiling water and boil until skins slip off easily—15 to 25 minutes depending on size.
- Skin and trim. Leave baby beets whole. Cut medium or larger beets in ½-inch cubes or slices.
- Pack hot in jar, adding 1 teaspoon salt per quart if desired. Cover with boiling water. Leave 1 inch head space.
- Remove air bubbles. Readjust head space.
- Wipe sealing edge of jar.
- Add and adjust lid.
- Sterilize at 10 pounds pressure* 30 minutes for quarts and pints.
- Cool canner before opening vent.
- Wait 2 minutes; remove lid.
- Remove jars from canner. Cool. Test for seals and store (directions in Chapter IV).

*For dial gauge, see altitude corrections, page 72.

Carrots

Hot pack, recommended method
- Select a suitable variety for canning, such as strains and hybrids of the Nantes variety which are coreless and rather small. Also good are Royal, Chantenay and Chantenay strains, Spartan Bonus, Danvers 126 and Bunny Bite (a baby carrot). Carrots should be young and sweet and canned the same day you harvest them.
- Prepare jars and lids.
- Wash and scrub in several changes of water until last rinse is clear; lift carrots from water after each washing.
- Peel, slice, dice or can whole.
- Cover with boiling water and boil 3 minutes.
- Pack hot in jar, adding 1 teaspoon salt per quart if desired. Cover with boiling water. Leave 1 inch head space.
- Remove air bubbles. Readjust head space.
- Wipe sealing edge of jar.
- Add and adjust lid.
- Sterilize at 10 pounds pressure* 30 minutes for quarts; 25 minutes for pints.
- Cool canner before opening vent.
- Wait 2 minutes; remove lid.
- Remove jars from canner. Cool. Test for seals and store (directions in Chapter IV).

Raw pack, acceptable method
- Follow all preceding steps except do not boil carrots. Pack raw in jar; cover with boiling water.
- Sterilize as for hot pack.

---

*For dial gauge, see altitude corrections, page 72.

Corn, Whole kernel

Hot pack, recommended method

- Pick sweet corn when kernels are full size, yet still milky and sweet, not starchy. Can immediately after harvesting. Most white varieties are not as good as yellow varieties for canning. Good varieties include NK 199 and Merit, both maturing in mid to late season. Iochief, although acceptable, is not as tender and sweet. Stylepack, Jubilee, Buttersweet and Tendersweet are also recommended varieties.
- Prepare jars and lids.
- Husk, remove silk and wash.
- Cut kernels from cob about two thirds depth.
- Place in kettle. Add 1 pint boiling water for each quart kernels. Heat to boiling.
- Pack hot loosely in jar, adding 1 teaspoon salt for each quart if desired. Cover with boiling water. Leave 1 inch head space.
- Remove air bubbles. Readjust head space.
- Wipe sealing edge of jar.
- Add and adjust lid.
- Sterilize at 10 pounds pressure* 1 hour 25 minutes for quarts; 55 minutes for pints.
- Cool canner before opening vent.
- Wait 2 minutes; remove lid.
- Remove jars from canner. Cool. Test for seals and store (directions in Chapter IV).

Raw pack, acceptable method

- Follow all preceding steps except do not boil corn. Pack raw loosely in jar; do not shake or press down. Cover with boiling water.
- Sterilize as for hot pack.

---

*For dial gauge, see altitude corrections, page 72.

Corn, Cream style
Hot pack, acceptable method
- There is higher risk of spoilage in cream style than in whole kernel corn. When heated, cream style becomes thick and pasty; this greatly slows down heat penetration during sterilization. Never use quart jars for canning cream style corn; follow all procedures strictly.
- Follow all preceding steps for whole kernel corn except scrape cob after cutting off kernels. Put kernels and scrapings in kettle, adding 1 pint boiling water per quart. Reheat to boiling; boil 3 minutes.
- Pack hot in pint jars only. Increase sterilizing time to 1 hour 25 minutes for pints.

Raw pack, acceptable method
- Follow all preceding steps for whole kernel corn except scrape cob after cutting off kernels. Pack kernels and scrapings raw in pint jars only. Do not shake or press down. Cover with boiling water.
- Increase sterilizing time to 1 hour 35 minutes for pints.

Special note
Sweet corn, a low-acid food, must be heat sterilized at 240°F (115°C)—that is, at 10 pounds pressure. But at temperatures higher than 240°F, sugar in sweet corn turns brown or caramelizes—this is what gives some canned corn an unattractive dark color.

Mushrooms
Hot pack, recommended method
- Select fresh mushrooms at peak maturity. Can promptly.
- Prepare jars and lids—pints or half-pints only.
- Soak mushrooms in cold water for 2 minutes; agitate water vigorously, several times, to remove adhering soil. Trim stems and discolored parts. Wash and rinse again in clean water. Can small mushrooms whole; slice larger ones.
- Cover with boiling water and boil 5 minutes.

*For dial gauge, see altitude corrections, page 72.

● Pack hot in jar, adding ½ teaspoon salt per pint if desired. For better color, add ⅛ teaspoon ascorbic acid per pint or use commercial antioxidant following package directions. Cover with boiling water. Leave 1 inch head space.

● Remove air bubbles. Readjust head space.

● Wipe sealing edge of jar.

● Add and adjust lid.

● Sterilize at 10 pounds pressure* 45 minutes for pints or half-pints.

● Cool canner before opening vent.

● Wait 2 minutes; remove lid.

● Remove jars from canner. Cool. Test for seals and store (directions in Chapter IV).

Peas

Hot pack, recommended method

● Select varieties suitable for canning. Little Marvel is an excellent small-seeded, small-podded variety; however, removing small seeds takes time. Progress No. 9 is a good large-seeded variety containing 4 to 6 seeds per pod. Lincoln, Green Arrow and Greater Progress are also recommended for canning. Pick peas when pods are bright green, moderately filled, young, sweet, not starchy. Can the same day.

● Prepare jars and lids.

● Wash, shell peas and wash again.

● Heat peas in blancher basket submerged in boiling water; boil 3 to 5 minutes.

● Pack hot, loosely in jar, adding 1 teaspoon salt per quart if desired. Cover with boiling water. Leave 1 inch head space.

● Remove air bubbles. Readjust head space.

● Wipe sealing edge of jar.

● Add and adjust lid.

● Sterilize at 10 pounds pressure* 40 minutes for quarts and pints.

*For dial gauge, see altitude corrections, page 72.

- Cool canner before opening vent.
- Wait 2 minutes; remove lid.
- Remove jars from canner. Cool. Test for seals and store (directions in Chapter IV).

Raw pack, acceptable method
- Follow all preceding steps except do not boil peas. Pack raw, loosely in jar; do not shake or press down. Cover with boiling water.
- Sterilize as for hot pack.

Potatoes, Cubed
Hot pack, recommended method
- Select firm, mature boiling potatoes such as Kennebec, Katahdin and Russet Burbank.
- Prepare jars and lids.
- Scrub potatoes. Pare and cut into ½-inch cubes. To prevent darkening, cut directly into brine made with 1 teaspoon salt per quart of water. Drain and rinse.
- Heat in blancher basket submerged in boiling water; boil 2 minutes.
- Pack hot in jar, adding 1 teaspoon salt per quart if desired. Cover with boiling water. Leave 1 inch head space.
- Remove air bubbles. Readjust head space.
- Wipe sealing edge of jar.
- Add and adjust lid.
- Sterilize at 10 pounds pressure* 40 minutes for quarts; 35 minutes for pints.
- Cool canner before opening vent.
- Wait 2 minutes; remove lid.
- Remove jars from canner. Cool. Test for seals and store (directions in Chapter IV).

*For dial gauge, see altitude corrections, page 72.

Potatoes, Whole
Hot pack, recommended method
- Follow all steps for Cubed Potatoes except choose potatoes 1 to 1½ inches in diameter.
- Increase blanching time to 10 minutes.
- Sterilize at 10 pounds pressure* 40 minutes for quarts; 30 minutes for pints.

Pumpkin or Winter Squash, Strained
Hot pack, recommended method
- Use firm, mature vegetable.
- Prepare jars and lids.
- Wash. Cut in half, remove seeds, pare and cut into 1-inch cubes.
- Place in kettle with just enough water to cover; simmer until tender, about 25 minutes.
- Press through a sieve or food mill.
- Simmer until heated through; stir to prevent sticking.
- Pack hot in jar. Leave 1 inch head space. Do not add liquid.
- Remove air bubbles. Readjust head space.
- Wipe sealing edge of jar.
- Add and adjust lid.
- Sterilize at 10 pounds pressure* 1 hour 20 minutes for quarts; 1 hour 5 minutes for pints.
- Cool canner before opening vent.
- Wait 2 minutes; remove lid.
- Remove jars from canner. Cool. Test for seals and store (directions in Chapter IV).

*For dial gauge, see altitude corrections, page 72.

Spinach and other Greens

Hot pack, recommended method

- Leafy greens tend to pack together, which slows down heat penetration during sterilization. Follow directions very carefully.
- Select young tender greens. Suitable varieties of spinach include Winter Bloomsdale, Long Standing Bloomsdale, Viking, Packer, Resistoflag, Viroflag, America, Early Hybrid #7, Hybrid #424, Hybrid #612. Can immediately after harvest.
- Discard decayed greens, tough stems and midribs. Wash very thoroughly in several changes of water until all soil is removed. Lift greens from water after each wash.
- Heat in blancher basket submerged in boiling water, just until wilted.
- Pack hot, loosely in jar, adding 1 teaspoon salt per quart if desired. Cover with boiling water. Leave 1 inch head space.
- Remove air bubbles. Readjust head space.
- Wipe sealing edge of jar.
- Add and adjust lid.
- Sterilize at 10 pounds pressure* 1 hour 30 minutes for quarts; 1 hour 10 minutes for pints.
- Cool canner before opening vent.
- Wait 2 minutes; remove lid.
- Remove jars from canner. Cool. Test for seals and store (directions in Chapter IV).

---

*For dial gauge, see altitude corrections, page 72.

Summer Squash

Hot pack, recommended method

- Select young, tender squash. Yellow varieties recommended for canning include Seneca Prolific, Seneca Butterbar, Goldban, Dixie and Golden Swan; green varieties include Zucchini Elite, Seneca Zucchini, Black Jack and Ambassador. Can the same day harvested.
- Wash but do not pare. Trim ends. Cut to make pieces of uniform size—½-inch slices or larger pieces such as quarters or halves.
- Heat in blancher basket submerged in boiling water; boil 2 to 3 minutes.
- Pack hot in jar, adding 1 teaspoon salt per quart if desired. Cover with boiling water. Leave 1 inch head space.
- Remove air bubbles. Readjust head space.
- Wipe sealing edge of jar.
- Add and adjust lid.
- Sterilize at 10 pounds pressure* 40 minutes for quarts; 30 minutes for pints.
- Cool canner before opening vent.
- Wait 2 minutes; remove lid.
- Remove jars from canner. Cool. Test for seals and store (directions in Chapter IV).

---

*For dial gauge, see altitude corrections, page 72.

MEAT AND POULTRY

Chicken or Rabbit

Hot pack, recommended method

- If you want to can meat on bones, cook meaty pieces until medium done. If you want to can meat only, cook until meat is done and remove from bones. Skim broth thoroughly to remove all fat.
- Prepare jars and lids.
- Pack meat loosely in jar, adding 1 teaspoon salt per quart if desired. Cover with boiling broth. Leave 1 to 1¼ inches head space.
- Remove air bubbles. Readjust head space.
- Wipe sealing edge of jar.
- Add and adjust lid.
- Sterilize at 10 pounds pressure* as follows: Meat with bones, 1 hour 15 minutes for quarts; 1 hour 5 minutes for pints. Meat without bones, 1 hour 30 minutes for quarts; 1 hour 15 minutes for pints.
- Cool canner before opening vent.
- Wait 2 minutes; remove lid.
- Remove jars from canner. Cool. Test for seals and store (directions in Chapter IV).

Raw pack, recommended method

- Follow all preceding steps for hot pack with these changes:
- Pack raw meaty pieces loosely in jar, leaving 1 to 1¼ inches head space.
- Set open filled jars on rack in kettle of hot water. Keep water level in pan 2 inches below jar tops.
- Put meat thermometer in center of one jar; cover kettle and heat slowly for about 1 hour 15 minutes or until thermometer registers 170°F (77°C). This drives air out of meat so vacuum will be formed in jars after heat sterilization and cooling.

---

*For dial gauge, see altitude corrections, page 72.

- Remove jars from kettle. Remove thermometer. Add 1 teaspoon salt per quart if desired. Do not add liquid—meat makes its own broth during sterilization.
- Sterilize at 10 pounds pressure,* same time as hot pack.

Chopped Meat
Beef, lamb, veal, venison
Hot pack, recommended method
- Prepare jars and lids.
- Shape ground meat into patties or balls, or can without shaping.
- Cook in oven or skillet until nearly done. Drain to remove excess fat.
- Pack hot in jar, adding 1 teaspoon salt per quart if desired. Cover with boiling broth or water. Leave 1 to 1¼ inches head space.
- Remove air bubbles. Readjust head space.
- Wipe sealing edge of jar.
- Add and adjust lid.
- Sterilize at 10 pounds pressure* 1 hour 30 minutes for quarts; 1 hour 15 minutes for pints.
- Cool canner before opening vent.
- Wait 2 minutes; remove lid.
- Remove jars from canner. Cool. Test for seals and store (directions in Chapter IV).

*For dial gauge, see altitude corrections, page 72.

Meat, Strips or Cubes
Beef, lamb, pork, veal, venison
Hot pack, recommended method
- Prepare jars and lids.
- Carefully cut meat from bones and remove visible fat. Cut into pieces such as jar-length strips (with grain of meat running height of jar) or smaller, stew-size pieces.
- Pre-cook meat until medium done by roasting, stewing or browning in a small amount of fat.
- Drain off excess fat.
- Pack hot, loosely in jar, adding 1 teaspoon salt per quart if desired. Cover with boiling meat juices and/or boiling water. Leave 1 to 1¼ inches head space.
- Remove air bubbles. Readjust head space.
- Wipe sealing edge of jar.
- Add and adjust lid.
- Sterilize at 10 pounds pressure* 1 hour 30 minutes for quarts; 1 hour 15 minutes for pints.
- Cool canner before opening vent.
- Wait 2 minutes; remove lid.
- Remove jars from canner. Cool. Test for seals and store (directions in Chapter IV).

Raw pack, recommended method
- Follow preceding steps for hot pack with these changes:
- Pack raw meat loosely in jar, leaving 1 to 1¼ inches head space.
- Set open filled jars on rack in kettle of hot water. Keep water level in pan 2 inches below jar tops.
- Put meat thermometer in center of one of the jars; cover kettle and heat slowly for about 1 hour 15 minutes or until thermometer registers 170°F (77°C). This drives air out of meat so vacuum will be formed in jars after heat sterilization and cooling.
- Remove jars from kettle. Remove thermometer. Add 1 teaspoon salt per quart if desired. Do not add liquid—meat makes its own broth during sterilization.
- Sterilize at 10 pounds pressure,* same time as hot pack.

---

*For dial gauge, see altitude corrections, page 72.

Sausage

Hot pack, recommended method

- Prepare jars and lids.
- Shape into patties or balls, or can without shaping.
- Cook sausage until lightly browned.
- Drain to remove excess fat.
- Pack hot in jar. Cover with boiling water. Leave 1 to 1¼ inches head space.
- Remove air bubbles. Readjust head space.
- Wipe sealing edge of jar.
- Add and adjust lid.
- Sterilize at 10 pounds pressure* 1 hour 30 minutes for quarts; 1 hour 15 minutes for pints.
- Cool canner before opening vent.
- Wait 2 minutes; remove lid.
- Remove jars from canner. Cool. Test for seals and store (directions in Chapter IV).

Tomato Sauce with Meat
for Spaghetti or Lasagna

Hot pack, recommended method

- Prepare tomato sauce, following directions in Chapter V.
- Brown ground meat; drain to remove excess fat. Combine with hot sauce.
- Pack hot in jar; leave 1 inch head space.
- Remove air bubbles. Readjust head space.
- Wipe sealing edge of jar.
- Add and adjust lid.
- Sterilize at 10 pounds pressure* 1 hour 15 minutes for quarts; 1 hour for pints.
- Cool canner before opening vent.
- Wait 2 minutes; remove lid.
- Remove jars from canner. Cool. Test for seals and store (directions in Chapter IV).

---

*For dial gauge, see altitude corrections, page 72.

CHAPTER VII

Home Canning Wrap-Up

Any mistakes you make in canning procedures will give you a less than perfect product. At best, your food may simply be less attractive than it should be—with poor color, texture and flavor. At worst, the food will be spoiled—unfit or even unsafe to eat.

This chapter gives you the standards to judge your own home canned food, describes some of the reasons for color changes and lid failures, and reviews the errors that may result in a poor product, or a spoiled product.

Check food for safety before you serve it

Every home canner (and everyone who accepts home canned food from friends) should be alert to the signs of spoilage.

Before you open any jar, look carefully at jar and lid. Is the lid still sealed? Or has liquid leaked from the jar? Is the lid still concave in the center—still drawn down by vacuum in the jar? Or is it bulging? If it's flat or slightly rounded—no longer concave—that's the beginning of bulging. Does the food itself, and the liquid, look normal? Are there any signs of fermenting inside the jar?

Do not use any food from a jar that has leaked, or has a broken seal or lid that has bulged, or has bubbles rising, which indicates it is fermenting.

Be alert when opening a jar—not all spoilage is evident by examination of the jar and lid. (Review the section on detecting spoilage, pages 19-20.)

Is there a spurting or rushing out of liquid? Is there an unnatural or off odor coming from the jar? Does the food look abnormally soft or cloudy? Spurting or off odors or suspicious appearance are definite signs that spoilage has taken place in the jar. Heating intensifies off odors. DO NOT TASTE SUCH FOOD. Destroy entire contents of jar.

For safety's sake

Most books and bulletins on home canning tell you to *boil home canned vegetables, meats and poultry at least 10 minutes before tasting and/or serving.* This has been the cardinal rule of home canners for generations—a prudent safeguard against the possibility *Clostridium botulinum* may have grown in low-acid foods which were improperly canned or not adequately sterilized. Boiling such foods vigorously for 10 minutes (covered or uncovered) is long enough to destroy the neuro-toxin responsible for botulism, if present.

This precautionary boiling is definitely recommended unless you are absolutely sure that your equipment is reliable and that you followed recommended procedures to the letter:

• Foods were canned in a pressure canner, following all directions for its use.

• Foods were heat sterilized for the recommended length of time for the food, the method of pack (hot or raw) and the size jar.

• Pressure gauge was accurate.

• Air was completely exhausted from the canner so pressure indicator was accurate.

• Necessary altitude corrections were made if canning with a dial-gauge canner at altitudes 2000 feet or higher.

• Proper pressure was maintained throughout heat sterilization time.

Signs of top-quality food

Top-quality home canned foods have rich, jewel-like colors characteristic of the food canned. Colors are those of well-prepared foods ready to be served; food does not look fresh or uncooked, nor does it look overcooked. Light-colored foods should have no signs of darkening.

Fruits and vegetables should be free of stems, cores, seeds or pieces of skin, and should be of uniform size, shape and color. Vegetables look young and tender, not old and starchy. Fruits look neither underripe and hard, nor overripe and mushy. Fruit is not floating to tops of jars and there is no severe separation of juices. For most foods, liquid should cover solid food in the jar and there should be a good proportion of solid to liquid.

The jars should be filled to the proper level, with head space of ¼ inch for juice, sauces and purees without meat; ½-inch head space for fruits; 1 inch for vegetables; 1 to 1¼ inches for meats.

There are several reasons for loss or apparent loss of liquid in canning jars. If pressure fluctuated during heat sterilization, or if it was reduced too quickly during cooling, this might force liquid from jars. If the food is raw packed, exhausting the air still in food tissues will also result in reduced volume and lower level of liquid. Leaving too little head space or packing food too tightly are other causes; it may also be characteristic of a particular jar lid.

Color Changes in Food

Treating fresh-cut foods to prevent darkening has been covered in Chapter IV. In addition to darkening, other color changes may occur in canned foods.

Carrots, peaches, apricots, squash and tomatoes contain *carotenoids*, a group of yellow, orange, orange-red or red pigments which do not dissolve in water. Thus, in canned food, color loss is slight. However, *carotenoids* do fade when heated in the presence of oxygen. For this reason, hot packing is recommended because it helps remove oxygen from food tissues.

Green pigments in immature fruits and all green vegetables are called *chlorophylls*. These pigments are unstable when heated. When green beans are first heated, for example, the green color brightens. You observe this when you blanch the vegetable before freezing or canning. However, as heating continues, the bright green color changes to olive green, and finally to a dull, greenish brown. The process of color changes in green vegetables is slowed somewhat by cooking in open kettles. During initial heating of fresh green vegetables, volatile acids (vaporized form of acids) are driven off from the tissue. If these volatile acids are trapped under a lid in a pan or jar, they speed up undesirable changes in color.

Some people add soda to canning water to retain better green color, but it destroys heat-sensitive vitamins and softens food texture, and is not recommended. Use of hot packing and pressure canning helps to limit these color changes.

Most red, blue and purple colors in cherries, most small berries, grapes and beets belong to a group of pigments known as *anthocyanins*. These pigments are water soluble; they dissolve readily if cell walls of fruits and beets are crushed or bruised before washing and canning. Cooking beets with skins, short tops and roots, helps retain color. Cooking and canning such foods in slightly acid water, or water acidified with a commercial antioxidant, citric acid or vinegar, also helps retain natural colors of these pigments. Alkaline water and even detergent residues on jars and cookware will change these red, blue and purple pigments to blues and greens.

Anthoxanthins and *flavones* are yellowish pigments normally invisible. They are contained in the white flesh cells of most apples, potatoes, onions, cauliflower and white cabbage. If you can these foods in naturally hard or softened water, they become yellow or cream colored. You can prevent such color changes by adding a very small quantity of cream of tartar or citric acid to the water used in cooking and canning these foods.

Since some natural pigments in light-colored fruits are light-sensitive and may darken even when canned, a dark, relatively cool storage area is recommended.

Reasons for spoilage of canned food

Canning is a precise and careful procedure; even small mistakes can result in food that's not as good as it should be.

If you are in any way disappointed in your canned food, run through this check list of possible errors:

CLEANLINESS

- Jars not perfectly clean and free of detergent residue.
- Jars not sterilized for such foods as jams and pickles, which spend less than 15 minutes in a boiling water canner.
- Food not clean, or not adequately trimmed to remove decayed or bruised spots.
- Food not freshly picked—not in prime condition.
- Food not peeled.

PREPARING AND PACKING FOOD

- Use of too little salt in fermenting cucumbers or other vegetables prior to canning.
- Use of homemade vinegar in pickling vegetables prior to canning. Standard vinegar of 5 percent acid strength is recommended.
- Use of open kettle canning—no longer recommended.
- Jars not standard canning jars . . . or jars not free of nicks or hairline cracks or other imperfections on sealing edge.
- Packing or filling food too tightly in jars.
- Failure to clean sealing surface of jar before adding lid.
- Failure to follow manufacturer's directions for preparing and adjusting lid.

HEAT STERILIZING

- Failure to begin with and maintain proper water level in a boiling water canner.
- Failure to use a pressure canner to sterilize low-acid foods.
- Failure to exhaust pressure canner sufficiently.
- Insufficient heat sterilization time for the specific food, method of pack and size of jar.
- Errors in timing heat sterilization.
- Failure to maintain proper heat under the canner throughout the entire heat sterilization time.
- Use of pressure canner with inaccurate pressure gauge or faulty seal.
- Failure to increase heat sterilization time when canning at altitudes above 1000 feet in boiling water canner; or to increase pressure if using dial gauge canner at altitudes above 2000 feet.

• Failure to correct errors due to loss or interrupted supply of gas or electricity during heat sterilization.

SEALING
• Failure to use standard canning jar with screw band that fits it.
• Sealing edge of jar uneven, or not free of nicks and/or hairline cracks.
• Screw band rusty or damaged, or not of recommended type.
• Screw band not tightened as directed, or other directions from lid manufacturer not followed.
• Defects in the lid itself—gaps in sealing compound, or lid not manufactured in accordance with recommended metal and gasket compound specifications.
• Lids not new—you should never re-use lids.
• Sealing edge of jar not wiped clean of food, seeds, grease or syrup.
• Overfilling jars or use of raw pack, either or both of which may cause bits of food tissue to lodge between sealing surface of lid and jar during sterilization. These bits of food may then act as a wick, allowing air to leak slowly into jar with resulting loss of seal.
• Inadequate heat sterilization—not enough to effect a vacuum seal.

Easy Reference Chart for Home Canning

(For detailed directions, see reference page)

Food Product	Type Pack	Preparation
APPLES	Hot	Use firm, ripe fruit. Wash, pare, core. Treat to prevent darkening. Rinse. Boil 5 minutes in syrup or water. Pack hot in jar. Cover with boiling syrup or water.
APPLESAUCE	Hot	Use firm, ripe fruit. Wash, pare, core. Treat to prevent darkening. Rinse. Simmer in small amount of water until tender. Sweeten to taste, if desired. Reheat to boiling. Pack hot in jar.
APRICOTS	Hot	Use firm, ripe fruit. Wash, peel, halve, pit. Treat to prevent darkening. Rinse. Heat to boiling in syrup or water. Pack, cavity side down, in jar. Cover with boiling syrup or water.
APRICOTS	Raw	Use firm, ripe fruit. Wash, peel, halve, pit. Treat to prevent darkening. Rinse. Pack raw in jar, cavity side down. Cover with boiling syrup or water.
ASPARAGUS	Hot	Use tender spears, freshly picked. Wash, break off tough ends and trim off scales. Cut in 1-inch pieces or can as whole spears. Boil 2 to 3 minutes. Add 1 teaspoon salt per quart if desired. Pack hot in jar. Cover with boiling water.
ASPARAGUS	Raw	Use tender spears, freshly picked. Wash, break off tough ends and trim off scales. Cut in 1-inch pieces or can as whole spears. Add 1 teaspoon salt per quart if desired. Pack raw, tightly in jar without crushing. Cover with boiling water.
BEANS Lima	Hot	Use tender beans, freshly picked. Wash, shell, rinse. Boil 3 minutes. Add 1 teaspoon salt per quart if desired. Pack hot, loosely in jar. Cover with boiling water.

Acid foods, light type; **low-acid foods, heavy type**

Head Space	Sterilization Method	Sterilization QUARTS	Time PINTS	Detailed Directions
½ inch	boiling water	20 minutes	15 minutes	page 48
¼ inch	boiling water	15 minutes	15 minutes	page 49
½ inch	boiling water	25 minutes	20 minutes	page 49
½ inch	boiling water	30 minutes	25 minutes	page 50
1 inch	pressure canner at 10 pounds pressure	30 minutes	25 minutes	page 73
1 inch	pressure canner at 10 pounds pressure	30 minutes	25 minutes	page 73
1 inch	pressure canner at 10 pounds pressure	50 minutes	40 minutes	page 73

For time and pressure changes at high altitudes, see pages 46 and 72

Easy Reference Chart for Home Canning

(For detailed directions, see reference page)

Food Product	Type Pack	Preparation
BEANS Lima	Raw	Use tender beans, freshly picked. Wash, shell, rinse. Add 1 teaspoon salt per quart if desired. Pack raw, very loosely in jar—do not press or shake down. Cover with boiling water.
BEANS Snap, Green or Wax	Hot	Use tender beans, easy to snap. Wash carefully. Trim ends. Cut or snap into 1½-inch pieces. Boil 3 minutes. Add 1 teaspoon salt per quart if desired. Pack hot loosely in jar.· Cover with boiling water.
BEANS Snap, Green or Wax	Raw	Use tender beans, easy to snap. Wash carefully. Trim ends. Cut or snap into 1½-inch pieces. Add 1 teaspoon salt per quart if desired. Pack raw, tightly in jar. Cover with boiling water.
BEETS	Hot	Use fresh beets, 1 to 1½ inches in diameter. Sort for size; trim, leaving 1 inch stem and root; wash and rinse well. Cover with boiling water; simmer 15 to 25 minutes or until skin slips off easily. Skin and trim. Leave baby beets whole; cut larger beets in ½-inch cubes or slices. Add 1 teaspoon salt per quart if desired. Pack hot in jar. Cover with boiling water.
BERRIES	Hot	Use firm, ripe berries. Sort, wash, drain well. Add ½ cup sugar to each quart fruit in kettle. Cover, bring to boil, stir gently. Pack hot in jar. Cover with boiling syrup from cooking.
BERRIES	Raw	Use firm, ripe berries. Sort, wash, drain well. Pack raw in jar. Shake down while filling Cover with boiling light syrup or water.
CARROTS	Hot	Use young, sweet, fresh carrots. Scrub well. Peel, slice, dice or leave whole. Boil 3 minutes. Add 1 teaspoon salt per quart if desired. Pack hot in jar. Cover with boiling water.
CARROTS	Raw	Use young, sweet, fresh carrots. Scrub well. Peel, slice, dice or leave whole. Add 1 teaspoon salt per quart if desired. Pack raw in jar. Cover with boiling water.

Acid foods, light type; low-acid foods, heavy type

Head Space	Sterilization Method	Sterilization QUARTS	Time PINTS	Detailed Directions
1 inch	pressure canner at 10 pounds pressure	50 minutes	40 minutes	page 74
1 inch	pressure canner at 10 pounds pressure	25 minutes	20 minutes	page 74
1 inch	pressure canner at 10 pounds pressure	25 minutes	20 minutes	page 74
1 inch	pressure canner at 10 pounds pressure	30 minutes	30 minutes	page 75
½ inch	boiling water	15 minutes	15 minutes	page 50
½ inch	boiling water	15 minutes	15 minutes	page 51
1 inch	pressure canner at 10 pounds pressure	30 minutes	25 minutes	page 76
1 inch	pressure canner at 10 pounds pressure	30 minutes	25 minutes	page 76

For time and pressure changes at high altitudes, see pages 46 and 72

Easy Reference Chart for Home Canning
(For detailed directions, see reference page)

Food Product	Type Pack	Preparation
CHERRIES	Hot	Use firm, ripe cherries. Wash, discard floaters. Remove stems; pit if desired. Add ½ cup sugar to each quart cherrries in kettle. (Add water if you did not remove pits.) Cover, bring to boil. Pack hot in jar. Cover with boiling syrup from cooking.
CHERRIES	Raw	Use firm, ripe cherries. Wash, discard floaters. Remove stems; pit if desired. Pack raw in jar. Shake down while filling. Cover with boiling syrup.
CHICKEN or RABBIT	Hot	Cook in broth, to medium doneness if canning with bone; or cook until done and remove from bones. Carefully skim fat from broth. Add 1 teaspoon salt per quart. Pack meat loosely in jar. Cover with boiling broth.
CHICKEN or RABBIT	Raw	Add 1 teaspoon salt per quart if desired. Pack meaty raw pieces loosely in jar. Set jar, uncovered, on a rack in a kettle of water; keep water level 2 inches below jar tops. Cover kettle and heat slowly 1 hour 15 minutes or until meat thermometer in jar registers 170°F (77°C). Remove jar from kettle. Add and adjust lid. Heat sterilize.
CORN Whole kernel	Hot	Use mature sweet corn, freshly picked. Husk, remove silks, wash. Cut kernels two-thirds depth from cobs. Add 1 pint boiling water to each quart kernels in kettle, heat to boiling. Add 1 teaspoon salt per quart if desired. Pack hot in jar. Cover with boiling water.
CORN Whole kernel	Raw	Use mature sweet corn, freshly picked. Husk, remove silks, wash. Cut kernels two-thirds depth from cobs. Add 1 teaspoon salt per quart if desired. Pack loosely in jar; do not shake or press down. Cover with boiling water.
CORN Cream style	Hot	Use mature sweet corn, freshly picked. Husk, remove silks, wash. Cut from cob and scrape cob. Add 1 pint boiling water for each quart cut corn in kettle; boil 3 minutes. Add ½ teaspoon salt per pint if desired. Pack hot *in pint jars only.*

Acid foods, light type; **low-acid foods, heavy type**

Head Space	Sterilization Method	Sterilization QUARTS	Time PINTS	Detailed Directions
½ inch	boiling water	15 minutes	15 minutes	page 51
½ inch	boiling water	25 minutes	20 minutes	page 52
1 to 1¼ inches	pressure canner at 10 pounds pressure	1 hour 15 minutes with bones 1 hour 30 minutes without bones	1 hour 5 minutes 1 hour 15 minutes	page 84
1 to 1¼ inches	pressure canner at 10 pounds pressure	1 hour 15 minutes with bones 1 hour 30 minutes without bones	1 hour 5 minutes 1 hour 15 minutes	page 84
1 inch	pressure canner at 10 pounds pressure	1 hour 25 minutes	55 minutes	page 77
1 inch	pressure canner at 10 pounds pressure	1 hour 25 minutes	55 minutes	page 77
1 inch	pressure canner at 10 pounds pressure	----	1 hour 25 minutes	page 78

For time and pressure changes at high altitudes, see pages 46 and 72

Easy Reference Chart for Home Canning
(For detailed directions, see reference page)

Food Product	Type Pack	Preparation
CORN Cream style	Raw	Use mature sweet corn, freshly picked. Husk, remove silks, wash. Cut from cob and scrape cob. Add ½ teaspoon salt per pint if desired. Pack raw *in pint jars only.* Cover with boiling water.
CUCUMBERS Pickled		Use pickling variety, freshly picked, firm, not yellowed, of size desired. Scrub with brush, wash, slice ⅛ inch from both ends. Follow recipe; pack in jars, cover with boiling pickling syrup or brine.

FRUIT BUTTERS
  Apple,
  Peach, Pear,
  Plum
	Hot	Use firm, ripe fruit. Wash, remove skin and pits, cut in pieces. Simmer until soft. Put through sieve or food mill. Cook until thick enough to hold shape on spoon; stir to prevent sticking. Add 2 cups sugar to each quart pulp and cinnamon and ground cloves to taste. Simmer until thick enough to spread; stir to prevent sticking. Pack hot in sterilized jars.

FRUIT JUICES	Hot	Use juicy, flavorful ripe fruit. Wash, remove pits, crush. Heat to simmer; strain through cloth bag. Add 1 cup sugar per gallon if desired. Reheat to simmer; pack hot in jar.
FRUIT PUREES	Hot	Use firm, ripe fruit. Wash, remove skins and pits, cut in pieces. Simmer until soft. Put through sieve or food mill. Add sugar to taste. Simmer to desired consistency. Pack hot in jar.
JAMS, JELLIES PRESERVES	Hot	Use firm, well-ripened fruit. Wash and prepare as directed in recipe, removing skins and peels. Sterilize jars. Follow recipe using commercial pectin. Pack hot in jars. Add and adjust lids. Heat sterilize.
MEATS Chopped	Hot	Shape into balls or patties, or can without shaping. Cook in oven or skillet until nearly done. Drain to remove excess fat. Add 1 teaspoon salt per quart if desired. Cover with boiling broth or water.

Acid foods, light type; **low-acid foods, heavy type**

Head Space	Sterilization Method	Sterilization QUARTS	Time PINTS	Detailed Directions
1 inch	pressure canner at 10 pounds pressure	----	1 hour 35 minutes	page 78
¼ inch	boiling water	Follow recipe; see detailed directions		page 65
¼ inch	boiling water	----	10 minutes (same for half-pints)	page 52
¼ inch	boiling water	15 minutes	15 minutes	page 53
¼ inch	boiling water	15 minutes	15 minutes	page 53
⅛ inch	boiling water	5 minutes	5 minutes	page 54
1 to 1¼ inches	pressure canner at 10 pounds pressure	1 hour 30 minutes	1 hour 15 minutes	page 85

For time and pressure changes at high altitudes, see pages 46 and 72

Easy Reference Chart for Home Canning

(For detailed directions, see reference page)

Food Product	Type Pack	Preparation
MEATS Strips Cubes	Hot	Cut from bone; remove visible fat. Cut in pieces. Cook to medium doneness by roasting, stewing or browning. Remove excess fat. Add 1 teaspoon salt per quart if desired. Pack hot, loosely in jar. Cover with boiling meat juices or boiling water.
MEATS Strips Cubes	Raw	Cut from bone; remove visible fat. Cut in pieces. Add 1 teaspoon salt per quart if desired. Pack raw meat loosely in jar. Set jar, uncovered, on rack in kettle of water; keep water level 2 inches below jar top. Cover kettle and heat slowly 1 hour 15 minutes or until meat thermometer in jar registers 170°F (77°C). Remove jar from kettle. Add and adjust lid. Heat sterilize.
MUSHROOMS	Hot	Use mushrooms at peak maturity, freshly picked. Soak 2 minutes, agitating water several times to remove soil. Trim stems and discolored parts. Wash again and rinse. Leave small mushrooms whole; slice larger ones. Boil 5 minutes. Add ½ teaspoon salt per pint if desired and commercial antioxidant or ⅛ teaspoon ascorbic acid for better color. Pack hot in pint jars only. Cover with boiling water.
PEAS	Hot	Use bright green moderately-filled pods; young, sweet, freshly picked. Wash, shell and wash again. Boil 3 to 5 minutes. Add 1 teaspoon salt per quart if desired. Pack hot loosely in jar. Cover with boiling water.
PEAS	Raw	Use bright green moderately-filled pods; young, sweet, freshly picked. Wash, shell, and wash again. Add 1 teaspoon salt per quart if desired. Pack raw in jar—do not shake or press down. Cover with boiling water.
PEACHES	Hot	Use firm, ripe fruit. Wash, remove skins, halve, pit. Treat to prevent darkening. Rinse. Heat to boiling in syrup or water to cover. Pack hot in jar, cavity side down. Cover with boiling liquid.

Acid foods, light type; **low-acid foods, heavy type**

Head Space	Sterilization Method	Sterilization QUARTS	Time PINTS	Detailed Directions
1 to 1¼ inches	pressure canner at 10 pounds pressure	1 hour 30 minutes	1 hour 15 minutes	page 86
1 to 1¼ inches	pressure canner at 10 pounds pressure	1 hour 30 minutes	1 hour 15 minutes	page 86
1 inch	pressure canner at 10 pounds pressure	----	45 minutes (same for half-pints)	page 78
1 inch	pressure canner at 10 pounds pressure	40 minutes	40 minutes	page 79
1 inch	pressure canner at 10 pounds pressure	40 minutes	40 minutes	page 80
½ inch	boiling water	25 minutes	20 minutes	page 54

For time and pressure changes at high altitudes, see pages 46 and 72

Easy Reference Chart for Home Canning
(For detailed directions, see reference page)

Food Product	Type Pack	Preparation
PEACHES	Raw	Use firm, ripe fruit. Wash, remove skins, halve, pit. Treat to prevent darkening. Rinse. Pack raw in jar, cavity side down. Cover with boiling syrup or water.
PEARS	Hot	Use firm, ripe fruit. Wash, pare, halve, core. Treat to prevent darkening. Rinse. Heat to boiling in syrup or water to cover. Pack hot in jar, cavity side down. Cover with boiling liquid.
PEARS	Raw	Use firm, ripe fruit. Wash, pare, halve, core. Treat to prevent darkening. Rinse. Pack raw in jar, cavity side down. Cover with boiling syrup or water.
PICKLES Fruit and Vegetable	Hot	Wash and prepare fruits and/or vegetables as directed in recipe. Pack in jar, cover with boiling pickling syrup.
PINEAPPLE	Hot	Use firm, ripe pineapple. Wash, peel, cut in pieces or slices. Simmer in syrup, juice or water to cover until tender. Pack hot in jar. Cover with boiling liquid.
PINEAPPLE	Raw	Use firm, ripe pineapple. Wash, peel, cut in pieces or slices. Pack raw in jar. Cover with boiling juice, syrup or water.
PLUMS	Hot	Use firm, ripe fruit. Wash, prick with fork, heat to boiling in syrup or water. Pack hot in jar. Cover with boiling liquid.
PLUMS	Raw	Use firm, ripe fruit. Wash, prick with fork. Pack raw in jar. Cover with boiling syrup or water.
POTATOES Cubed	Hot	Use firm, mature boiling potatoes. Scrub, pare and cut into ½-inch cubes. Drop into brine (1 teaspoon salt dissolved in 1 quart water). Drain, rinse. Boil 2 minutes. Add 1 teaspoon salt per quart if desired. Pack hot in jar. Cover with boiling water.

Acid foods, light type; **low-acid foods, heavy type**

Head Space	Sterilization Method	Sterilization QUARTS	Time PINTS	Detailed Directions
½ inch	boiling water	30 minutes	25 minutes	page 55
½ inch	boiling water	25 minutes	20 minutes	page 56
½ inch	boiling water	30 minutes	25 minutes	page 56
¼ inch	boiling water	Follow recipe; see detailed directions		page 67
½ inch	boiling water	20 minutes	15 minutes	page 57
½ inch	boiling water	30 minutes	30 minutes	page 57
½ inch	boiling water	25 minutes	20 minutes	page 57
½ inch	boiling water	25 minutes	20 minutes	page 58
1 inch	pressure canner at 10 pounds pressure	40 minutes	35 minutes	page 80

For time and pressure changes at high altitudes, see pages 46 and 72

Easy Reference Chart for Home Canning
(For detailed directions, see reference page)

Food Product	Type Pack	Preparation
POTATOES Whole	Hot	Use boiling potatoes 1 to 2½-inches in diameter. Scrub, pare and drop in brine (1 teaspoon salt dissolved in 1 quart water). Drain and rinse. Boil 10 minutes. Add 1 teaspoon salt per quart if desired. Pack hot in jar. Cover with boiling water.
PRESERVES, see JAMS		
PUMPKIN	Hot	Use firm, mature vegetable. Remove seeds, pare, cut into 1-inch cubes. Boil in just enough water to cover until tender, about 25 minutes. Put through sieve or food press. Simmer until hot, stirring often. Pack hot in jar. Do not add liquid.
RABBIT, see CHICKEN		
RHUBARB	Hot	Use tender stalks. Wash, trim, cut in ½-inch pieces. Add ½ cup sugar per quart, let stand to draw out juices. Bring to a boil. Pack hot in jar.
SAUSAGE	Hot	Shape into patties or balls, or can without shaping. Cook until lightly browned; drain to remove excess fat. Pack hot in jar. Cover with boiling water.
SPINACH and other greens	Hot	Use young, tender leaves, freshly picked. Wash thoroughly. Discard decayed parts, tough stems and ribs. Heat in blancher until wilted. Add 1 teaspoon salt per quart if desired. Pack hot, loosely in jar. Cover with boiling water.
SQUASH Summer	Hot	Use young, tender squash, freshly picked. Wash but do not pare. Trim ends. Cut into ½-inch slices, or in other uniform-size pieces. Boil 2 to 3 minutes. Add 1 teaspoon salt per quart if desired. Pack hot in jar. Cover with boiling water.
SQUASH Winter, see PUMPKIN		

Acid foods, light type; low-acid foods, heavy type

Head Space	Sterilization Method	Sterilization QUARTS	Time PINTS	Detailed Directions
1 inch	pressure canner at 10 pounds pressure	40 minutes	35 minutes	page 81
1 inch	pressure canner at 10 pounds pressure	1 hour 20 minutes	1 hour 5 minutes	page 81
½ inch	boiling water	15 minutes	15 minutes	page 58
1 to 1¼ inches	pressure canner at 10 pounds pressure	1 hour 30 minutes	1 hour 15 minutes	page 87
1 inch	pressure canner at 10 pounds pressure	1 hour 30 minutes	1 hour 10 minutes	page 82
1 inch	pressure canner at 10 pounds pressure	40 minutes	30 minutes	page 83

For time and pressure changes at high altitudes, see pages 46 and 72

Easy Reference Chart for Home Canning

(For detailed directions, see reference page)

Food Product	Type Pack	Preparation
TOMATOES Whole or Quartered	Hot	Use firm, uniformly red tomatoes—not overly ripe, not green. Wash; trim away decayed spots. Remove skins by blanching. Remove cores; trim out green spots. Heat to boiling. Do not add water—stir to prevent sticking. Add 1 teaspoon salt per quart if desired. Pack hot in jar. Cover with boiling juice.
TOMATOES Whole or Quartered	Raw	Use firm, uniformly red tomatoes—not overly ripe, not green. Wash; trim away decayed spots. Remove skins by blanching. Remove cores; trim out green spots. Add 1 teaspoon salt per quart if desired. Pack raw in jar, pressing gently to fill space—or add boiling juice. Do not add water.
TOMATO JUICE	Hot	Use red-ripe tomatoes. Wash. Trim away bruised or decayed spots; remove stem ends and cut in pieces. Simmer until softened, stirring often. Put through sieve or food mill. Reheat until just boiling. Add 1 teaspoon salt per quart if desired. Fill hot in jar.
TOMATO SAUCE or PUREE (no vegetables or meat added)	Hot	Use red-ripe tomatoes. Wash. Trim away bruised or decayed spots; remove stem ends and cut in pieces. Simmer until softened, stirring often. Put through sieve or food mill. Simmer to desired consistency. Add ½ teaspoon salt per pint. Fill hot in jar.
TOMATO SAUCE or PUREE (with vegetables but no meat)	Hot	Use red-ripe tomatoes and firm, fresh vegetables. Wash. Trim away bruised or decayed spots; remove stem ends from tomatoes. Cut in pieces; simmer all ingredients until softened. Put through sieve or food mill. Simmer until pulp is thick (reduced to ½ volume).
TOMATO MEAT SAUCE	Hot	Prepare tomatoes as for tomato sauce. Brown ground meat; remove excess fat. Combine meat and sauce. Fill hot in jars.

Acid foods, light type; low-acid foods, heavy type

Head Space	Sterilization Method	Sterilization QUARTS	Time PINTS	Detailed Directions
½ inch	boiling water	45 minutes	35 minutes	page 60
½ inch	boiling water	50 minutes	40 minutes	page 60
¼ inch	boiling water	35 minutes	35 minutes	page 62
¼ inch	boiling water	----	35 minutes thin sauce 20 minutes thick sauce	page 62
¼ inch	boiling water	----	45 minutes (same for half-pints)	page 63
1 inch	pressure canner at 10 pounds pressure	1 hour 15 minutes	1 hour	page 87

For time and pressure changes at high altitudes, see pages 46 and 72

Glossary

Acid foods Foods which contain sufficient acids to result in a pH value of 4.5 or lower. All fruits; tomatoes; properly fermented or pickled vegetables; and jams, jellies, fruit preserves and fruit butters are acid foods.

Bacteria Large group of one-celled microorganisms widely distributed in nature. *See* Microorganisms.

Blancher Deep pot (4 to 8 quarts) with lid and perforated basket, preferably enamel or stainless steel. Basket is used to lower fruits and vegetables into boiling water, to loosen skins, or for heating (blanching) food to be hot packed.

Boiling water canner Large, deep porcelain or aluminum kettle with lid and jar rack. Used to sterilize acid foods.

Botulism Illness caused by eating toxin produced by growth of *Clostridium botulinum* bacteria in insufficiently sterilized, low-acid food, packaged in tightly-sealed jars, cans, or some vacuum-sealed films.

Brine Solution of salt and water.

Canning Method of preserving foods packed in containers, sterilized with heat and sealed airtight during cooling.

Canning salt Pure sodium chloride without the anti-caking or iodine additives in most table salt. It will usually be labeled canning or pickling salt.

Cling peach Type of peach with flesh that adheres to the seed, even when fully ripened.

Clostridium botulinum Bacteria native to soil, water and most fresh foods. Grows in absence of oxygen, in low-acid foods, at temperatures from 40° to 120° F (5° to 49° C), producing a neuro-toxin responsible for botulism. For canned food to be safe, both bacteria spores and vegetative cells must be destroyed by adequate heat sterilization.

Colander Perforated utensil for draining washed food.

Cold pack More correctly called raw pack—procedure of filling jars with washed, prepared, but unheated foods.

Concave Appearance of lid on jar of cooled canned food. As you sight across lid, center will be depressed or hollowed. This signals vacuum seal.

Enzymes A sub-microscopic biochemical substance in living food cells. When crushed or exposed to air, enzymes accelerate changes in food, texture and color; and increase loss of some vitamins. Mild heat—blanching or hot packing—easily destroys enzymes.

Exhausting Removal of air from within and around food tissue cells, or from jars and canners. Heating foods as in blanching and hot packing effectively exhausts air in foods. Exhausting or removing air from pressure canners is necessary to achieve true steam temperature associated with pressures used to heat sterilize canned food by this method.

Fermentation Chemical change in foods induced by bacteria, yeasts or molds. In canning, properly controlled fermentation by desirable, native bacteria results in conversion of sugars to lactic acid and other flavor components in sauerkraut and slow-process pickles. Undesirable fermentations resulting in spoilage may develop in canned foods which are not adequately heat sterilized.

Flat-sour Spoilage by certain bacteria whose growth increases acidiy of some canned food, without noticeable odors or gas. Spoiled cans appear normal, but food will have an unpleasant sourish-flavor. It is harmless if eaten. Spoilage may occur in canned tomatoes, sweet corn or other low-acid vegetables if jars are cooled insufficiently or stored at temperatures above 95° F (35° C).

Freestone peach Peach with flesh that separates easily from seed when fully ripe—desirable for home canning.

Gasket (for pressure canner) Ring of rubber (or other suitable material) which fits into a channel around canner lid. Gasket seals lid to canner when lid is locked in place. If gasket is improperly seated, if it is worn excessively from long use or neglect, or if dome lid is warped, there may be leakage when canner is pressurized.

Gauge (dial) Pressure *indicator* on some models of pressure canners. Pressure itself is controlled by regulating heat according to dial reading on gauge. While operating canner, constant monitoring is necessary to be sure canner sustains desired pressure.

Gauge (weighted) Pressure *controller* on some models of pressure canners. Counter-weighted gauge releases excess pressure automatically, signaling proper pressure throughout heat sterilization schedule by the audible jiggling of the weighted gauge. With proper use, it maintains accuracy indefinitely and needs no adjustment for altitude variations.

Head space Depth of air space between surface of food or liquid and underside of lid. Recommended head spaces vary with foods, methods of packing and heat sterilization.

Heat processing Literally means processing with heat, but in canning it usually means applying the amount of heat needed to sterilize canned foods. The term "heat sterilization" is preferred.

Heat-resistant Term applied to some forms of bacteria and molds that tolerate and survive unusually long periods of heating, whether in boiling water or at the higher temperatures achieved with steam in pressure canners.

Heat sterilization Time in minutes—either at temperature of boiling water or temperature achieved with steam pressure—needed to destroy all bacteria, molds and yeasts capable of growth in canned foods stored at temperatures below 95° F (35°C).

Heat sterilization schedule *Time*, in minutes, needed for heat sterilizing canned food at *specific temperature.*

Hermetic seal   Airtight or vacuum seal achieved when jars of sterilized food are cooled. Allows *absolutely* no transfer of air or microorganisms into or from jars.

Hot pack   Pre-heating or blanching of foods and filling hot in jars. For most foods, this is the recommended packing method because there are fewer seal failures; also food retains better color, more flavor and nutrients.

Jar lifter   Tool for lifting hot jars from boiling water or pressure canner.

Lids   Recommended vacuum-sealing or self-sealing lid consists of two pieces: A flat, enamel-coated metal lid which has a flexible center and a gasket or rubber sealing compound all around the rim on the enameled side. And a separate metal screw band. Lid is placed over sealing edge of glass jar, screw band is added and tightened firmly by hand. Properly used, this lid rarely fails.

One-piece lid similar to the two-piece lid is fully enamel-coated, with flexible center; there is a gasket substance or sealing compound around inside top rim.

Older-style zinc cap is one piece; it has screw threads and is lined with porcelain. This cap seals on the shoulder of jar, against a separate rubber ring; it must be retightened after sterilization to make the seal. No longer popular or recommended as it too often fails to make hermetic seal.

Lightning jar   Early type of home canning jar with a glass cap. Rubber ring is placed between jar and cap and tension applied with a wire bail to seal the jar. These jars often fail to form airtight seals and are not recommended.

Low-acid foods   Foods which contain very little acid and have a pH value of 4.6 or higher. Vegetables and all meats are low-acid foods, and when canned may support growth of *Clostridium botulinum* if not heat sterilized properly.

Mason jars   Jars tailored and made to standard specifications for use in home canning. As compared to one-trip jars, used to pack commercially-made products, glass walls of Mason jars are thicker, sealing surface is wider, screw threads and jar neck are of standardized dimensions; and jars withstand more heat shock without breaking.

Maximum thermometer   Tool for testing accuracy of dial-pressure gauge on pressure canners. Placed inside canner, it registers maximum temperature achieved and holds this reading, like a fever thermometer, until shaken down.

Microorganisms All bacteria, yeasts and molds are microorganisms. They are so extremely small they must be magnified 200 to 900 times to be seen. It would require from 10,000 to 25,000 microorganisms lined up end-to-end to measure one inch. When alive and in a suitable environment, microorganisms grow and reproduce rapidly. Many cause disease and illness and are, therefore, called human pathogens. Growth of others in food may be harmless but undesirable as they change the food's flavor and texture and may form obnoxious odors. Still other microorganisms produce desirable changes in food—for example, fermented Swiss cheese, Bleu cheese, sauerkraut and vinegars. All microorganisms capable of causing spoilage and possible hazards are destroyed in properly sealed canned food by use of proper heat sterilization, cooling and storage practices.

Mold Form of microorganism or fungus that grows on food, usually forming a visible cottony-looking mass that may be white or colored. Molds can grow on most fresh foods regardless of acidity; on some low-moisture foods such as breads and pastries; and in canned food not properly heat sterilized and sealed.

Mycotoxin Toxin produced by growth of some molds. Hazards to animals and humans from eating mycotoxins are being recognized. Molds are more likely to grow on such foods as jams, jellies and preserves prepared by open kettle canning and sealed with paraffin. Because of potential hazards of mycotoxins, these procedures are no longer recommended. For the same reason—to discourage mold growth—the peeling of apples, pears, peaches and apricots is recommended.

Open kettle canning Obsolete canning method. Food is supposedly cooked in covered kettle until heat sterilized, packed in sterilized jars and sealed, with no heat treatment after food is in jars. Open kettle canning is not a safe or recommended method for home preservation of foods.

Oven canning Unsafe canning method. Filled jars placed in dry heat of conventional or microwave ovens may explode; lids are less likely to seal, and because of uneven heating, jars may not be adequately heat sterilized. Not recommended.

Petcock   Mechanical valve on some old-model pressure canners. It is opened to exhaust air from heated canner; then petcock is closed manually to pressurize canner and heat sterilize jars of food.

pH   Term used to classify a precise measure of acidity and alkalinity. Values of pH range from 0 to 14. A value of 7 indicates food is neutral, being neither acid nor alkaline. As pH value increases from 7 to 14, food is increasingly more alkaline. As the pH value decreases from 7 to 0, food is increasingly more acid.

Pickling   Procedure to increase acidity in low-acid vegetables normally by use of vinegar. After proper pickling procedures are completed, foods are acid and need only heat sterilization in boiling water canner. Proper amounts of salt, sugars and spices are also added to impart desired texture and flavor to pickled foods before canning.

Press   Cone-shaped device for crushing and pressing juices from heated fruits or vegetables. A pestle, also cone-shaped, is rotated to squeeze food pieces against perforated surface of cone, pressing out juice but trapping seeds and skins.

Pressure canner   Deep, heavy metal kettle essential for heat sterilizing low-acid foods at temperatures of 228°F (109°C) or 240°F (115°C). It has a rack for jars and a lid which locks on, sealed airtight with a gasket. Lid has a device for exhausting air, a safety fuse and a dial or weighted pressure gauge.

Processing   Imprecise but much-used term in home canning; see definition for heat processing. Use of term "heat sterilization" is preferred.

Puree   Fruit or vegetable juice containing strained solids and thickened or concentrated by heating in an open kettle to desired consistency for sauces.

Putrifactive bacteria   Bacteria which grows in absence of air and causes spoilage, especially in foods high in protein. Spoiled foods have a putrid or obnoxious odor.

Raw pack Filling raw, unheated food in jars. Sometimes called cold pack.

Reprocess Imprecise term meaning to heat sterilize canned food a second time. This is done when lids fail to seal after heat sterilizing and cooling, or when heat is lost at any time during initial heat sterilization schedule.

Scalding Dipping tomatoes, peaches, apricots or nectarines in boiling water for a brief time to loosen skins. Depending on fruit, this takes 15 seconds to 1½ minutes or slightly longer. After scalding, fruit is cooled quickly in cold water. Skins will slip off easily.

Screw band A light-weight metal band designed to hold the flat jar lid in place during heat sterilization.

Self-sealing lid Descriptive of recommended two-piece lid. When used properly, it forms vacuum seal automatically as sterilized jar of food cools. You can hear the snap when vacuum seal develops. Leave screw band in place until jars are completely cool.

Spore Heat-resistant form of some bacteria and molds which, in a sense, is similar to plant seed. Spores are common to soil and some lake and sea water and, therefore, are found on most fresh foods. Like plant seeds, spores are a dormant form of life capable of surviving winters, droughts and periods of unavailable nutrients. Just as plant seeds germinate and produce new plants when placed in ideal growing conditions, spores will germinate, and produce new vegetative cells which grow and reproduce very rapidly. Spores are difficult to remove from fresh foods and therefore must be destroyed by proper heat sterilization of food being canned.

Sterilize To destroy all living forms of microorganisms capable of growth under ordinary environmental conditions during handling and storage of canned food.

Style of pack Form of canned food, such as: whole, sliced, diced, chunks, juice, puree, sauce or soup.

Syrup Light, medium or heavy sugar solution used in packing most fruits. Helps retain better color, flavor, texture and shape.

Temperature—pressure relationship Stable temperature of steam, free of air, achieved and maintained at elevated pressures. In home canning the following temperature—pressure relationships are recommended:

Gauge Pressure	Temperature	
5 pounds*	228°F	109°C
10 pounds*	240°F	115°C

*Pounds per square inch above atmosphere

Heat sterilization schedules for pressure canners are correctly applied only when all air is exhausted from canner before pressurizing.

Toxin Denotes a substance harmful if eaten. See mycotoxin and botulism.

Valve See petcock.

Vegetative cell The living form of microorganisms which grows and reproduces very rapidly in ideal conditions. Comparable in a sense to plants. See microorganisms for additional characteristics.

Yeast Group of microorganisms which reproduce by budding. See microorganisms for additional characteristics.

Zinc cap See description under Lids.

CONVERSION TABLES
English and Metric
Weight, Volume and Temperature Equivalents

Units of Weight
1 gram	0.035 ounces
1 kilogram	2.21 pounds
1 ounce	28.35 grams
1 pound	453.59 grams

Units of Volume
1 bushel	4 pecks
1 peck	8 quarts
1 gallon	4 quarts
1 quart	2 pints
	946.4 milliliters
	.95 liter
1 pint	2 cups
	2 gills
	8 fluid ounces
	236.6 milliliters
1 liter	1000 milliliters
	1.06 quarts
1 tablespoon	3 teaspoons
	½ fluid ounce
	14.8 milliliters
1 teaspoon	4.9 milliliters

Units of Temperature
212°F	100°C (Celsius or Centigrade)
32°F	0°C

To convert °F to °C:
$$°C = °F - 32 \,(5/9)$$
Example: If °F = 212 then °C = 212 – 32
= 180 ÷ 9 = 20 x 5 = 100°C

Index

124

ABOUT THE AUTHORS

LOUISE W. HAMILTON, R.D.

Louise W. Hamilton is a registered dietitian and professor of foods and nutrition with the Cooperative Extension Service of The Pennsylvania State University. A native of Ohio, she received her B.S. degree from Iowa State University and her M.A. degree in foods and nutrition from Penn State.

Miss Hamilton, with Gerald Kuhn, teaches a graduate credit course on home canning for county Extension home economists; she also conducts numerous canning workshops.

Miss Hamilton is active in professional organizations such as the Pennsylvania and American Dietetic Associations, the Pennsylvania and American Home Economics Associations and other Public Health and Nutrition Education groups. She is also a home gardener.

GERALD D. KUHN, Ph.D.

Gerald D. Kuhn is associate professor of food science with the Cooperative Extension Service of The Pennsylvania State University and conducts educational programs for fruit and vegetable processors and county Extension staff on food safety, processing and canning. With Louise Hamilton, he is researching the effectiveness of new jar lids.

A native of Indiana, he earned his B.S., M.S. and Ph.D. degrees from Purdue University. Prior to joining the Penn State staff he was on the Food Science staff, University of Florida, and taught at Purdue. Dr. Kuhn is a member of food science and agricultural honoraries, the National Institute of Food Technologists and the American Society for Horticultural Science.

Dr. Kuhn has a large vegetable garden and fruit orchard. In 1975, he and his wife canned 540 jars of fruits, vegetables, soups, jellies and jams, some of which are pictured on the cover of this book.

KAREN A. RUGH

Karen Ann Rugh, a communications specialist with the Cooperative Extension Service of The Pennsylvania State University, is responsible for press and television information. In addition, she teaches newswriting and direct mail techniques. She received her B.A. degree from Penn State.

Mrs. Rugh is a member of Women in Communications. She and her husband live in an historical home on a 100-acre Pennsylvania farm.